COMMUNING WITH MUSIC

Music . . . can name the unnameable and communicate the unknowable.

LEONARD BERNSTEIN

"Communing with Music is an excellent resource for those who are on a spiritual journey and yearning to make the most out of all their experiences."

~ *Spirituality & Health* Magazine

"*Communing with Music* offers a clear, concise overview of the different factors that combine to create a musical expression - tone, melody, harmony, rhythm, and color - and offers suggestions for training the ear and the mind to appreciate each. Exercises and guidelines are provided to help move the reader closer to Cantello's vision of 'absolute listening,' a state in which music can be a potent ally in creating relaxation, enhancing love and creativity, healing emotions, and even the physical body. Throughout the book, one senses Cantello's joy at living in an age with a smorgasbord of high-quality recordings available. He believes that this modern-day feast offers nourishment well beyond the words on its pages . . . The writing is clean, clear, and elegant . . ."

~ ANNE PYBURN, *Chronogram* Magazine

COMMUNING WITH
MUSIC

PRACTICING THE ART OF
CONSCIOUS LISTENING

MATTHEW CANTELLO

DeVorss Publications
Camarillo, California

Communing with Music
Copyright © 2004 by Matthew Cantello

Library of Congress Control Number: 2004055110
Print ISBN: 9780875169477
Ebook ISBN: 9780875169484

First Edition, 2004
Second Edition, 2023

Printed in the United States of America
DeVorss & Company, Publisher
P.O. Box 1389
Camarillo, California 93011-1389
www.devorss.com

Library of Congress Cataloging-in-Publication Data

Cantello, Matthew.
Communing with music: practicing the art of conscious listening/
Matthew Cantello. – 1st ed.
p. cm.
Includes bibliographical references (p.).
ISBN 0-87516-792-6
Music appreciation. I. Title.
MT6.C185.C66 2004
781.1'7—dc22
2004055110
ISBN: 0-87516-792-6

PUBLISHER'S NOTE:
Throughout this book, the author refers to multiple recording formats of which some may now be obsolete. Regardless of the medium or format, the techniques and guidelines described within are still pertinent to each recording and music selection.

CONTENTS

INTRODUCTION

Music is in a continual state of becoming.

AARON COPLAND

It's amazing how a seemingly ordinary experience can suddenly turn into a life-changing event, forever opening the door to a whole new way of seeing, hearing and feeling.

At least that was the way it happened for me one day, a number of years back.

Feeling overwhelmed by a hectic schedule, relationship difficulties and a gnawing sense of insecurity, I had promised myself the special opportunity of a day to do absolutely nothing—nowhere to go, no agenda whatsoever. I envisioned a solitary time of lounging about, reading poetry, or maybe even gazing purposelessly out of my living room window. I began the morning by easing over to the stereo system, as I often did, to put on a recording that a friend had loaned me—a collection of piano pieces by a turn-of-the-century French composer.

Throughout the day, the sound of the piano flowed through the speakers, filling the room with an exquisitely tender light.

After taking in each piece a number of times, I noticed that a particular cycle of nocturnes consistently stood apart from the rest. It seemed the poignant, longing nature of the sonorities struck a chord with the uneasiness I was feeling toward the mounting uncertainties in my life.

The day passed into evening, and the music had long since ended, but as I prepared for dinner, those nocturnes stayed with me somehow, leaving an imprint that I couldn't quite explain in words. It felt as if the sounds had managed to pry open a willing, receptive space within, an openness that was new to the sense of rigidity I had been carrying around for so long. Later, after going out for the evening and returning quite late, I was compelled to experience those nocturnes once again before bed. I felt the need to make contact with that mysterious beauty that seemed so rife with possibility. This time I felt intuitively that I should prepare for the experience in some way, not unlike one does for prayer or meditation, if only to put myself in the most open and receptive state possible. After trying some exercises to quiet my mind and body, I went upstairs, lay down in the darkness, and pressed the "play" button.

$$\mathcal{9}:$$

As the first notes entered the quiet stillness, I just knew that something very different was about to happen. The sound was incredibly alive with energy, conveying a manner of beauty beyond anything I encountered before. It seemed as if the melodies and harmonies were speaking directly to my soul, revealing unexplainable truths with what seemed like the voice of compassion itself. As I closed my eyes, trying desperately to absorb every bit of the music, I felt streams of loving energy beginning to well up from deep within. Time seemed to stand still, as each note opened further and further the tightness of my shielded heart. I felt I was becoming, what can only be described as one with the music—music so hauntingly beautiful that it awakened a realm of experience I didn't even know was possible. Instantly, the distress that had been lodged deep in my bones began to subside, and was replaced by the most ecstatic state of compassionate joy. Even after the music had faded gently away, I lay in silence half the night, dwelling in such a profound awareness of my inherent wholeness.

Looking back, that night was my first peak experience inspired by music—one of many to come. As a musician and a music teacher, I had long been familiar with the joys of music, but until that day I never fully understood its true evocative power. What a thrill to discover that simply opening oneself to the vibrations of musical sound could bring about such a transcendent experience! Ever since that time, I never considered music in the same way again. A new dimension opened in my life. Having had a taste of what music could evoke, I felt a keen desire to explore the breadth of its transformational potential. What range of experience could powerful music awaken from within? Could this potent form of energy be harnessed for healing and spiritual growth?

In setting out on my quest of musical discovery, I soon realized what a unique time it was to explore the healing potential of the musical experience. I was newly inspired by the wealth and availability of resources from which I could draw. Over time and through much experimentation, I began to synthesize more ancient practices and ideas with the benefit of modern technology and understanding. Charged with a revived sensitivity, I searched tirelessly for the most powerful music I could find, seeking to uncover those rare works whose secret formulas could manage to truly stir the soul. At the heart of my search was a decision to take the music very seriously; to experience it consciously, rather than passively, in an effort to bring about significant transformations of consciousness. As a musician, my primary role was most often the creating or composing of music. By changing positions and putting myself on the opposite end of the music equation I was free to focus exclusively on receiving sound. This stepping back allowed me to experience music with a different focus and intensity than ever before.

One of the most significant insights gained in the course of my explorations was the vital role of receptivity. As I became increasingly attuned to how state of mind, sensitivity and awareness affected my musical perception, it became necessary to search for ways to heighten receptivity—to attend to the inner world that I brought to each experience.

Eventually, it dawned on me that what I was essentially attempting to do was commune with the power and beauty of musical sound, as one might commune with a loved one or the wonders of the natural world. Yet in time, I also became aware that I was ultimately communing with much more than music per se. I began to see how uniting with the energy of music was essentially a vehicle for connecting with the spirit of the universe itself, a portal through which I could uncover my true nature.

Needless to say, my relationship with music soon developed into a much more spiritual practice. Now, you could say that music has become an ally in my journey in life. Utilized in partnership with the practices of my own spiritual path, there are so many ways that music deepens my experience of life. It heals and revitalizes me, connects me with the sacred, uncovers insights and leads me to ecstatic wholeness—so much so that it has given me the motivation to develop and offer this communing method so that I can share the incredible potential of music with others.

In the pages ahead we will explore how to "commune with music"—an innovative and thorough method that teaches how to enhance our lives with this exquisite power, even in the midst of our accelerating modern lives.

Our journey takes place on many levels by:

♭ Awakening a renewed awareness and appreciation of music and sound in our lives, and the many ways it can enhance our well being.

♭ Discovering the realm of "power music," and how to seek, gather and preserve our own collection (with an extensive list to explore in the Appendix, page 141).

♭ Learning how to practice "communing techniques," contemplative exercises that enable us to unite with, and therefore be transformed by, musical power.

♭ Heightening our receptivity to musical expression by strengthening musical sensitivity and developing auditory awareness.

♭ Learning how to optimize our communing experiences with preparation and the benefit of modern audio technology.

Be assured that you don't have to be formally trained in music to receive its benefits. Whatever our experience or background, we can learn how to utilize the power of music to enhance our lives. For those with musical experience, this method enables us to see and experience music anew, to experience new life through our musical world.

In cultivating a meaningful connection with the valuable resource of music, we start with gaining an appreciation for the gift of sound.

COMMUNING WITH MUSIC

CHAPTER ONE

THE GIFT OF SOUND

So what exactly is this phenomenon we call *music*, the invisible, mysterious force that can heal and awaken the human soul? Surely this question has been pondered throughout the ages. Yet, whatever our exposition—be it practical or mystical—we must concede that music is fundamentally born of sound, the same stuff that fashions whispers, thunderclaps and all the other sonic perceptions of our human experience. What escapes most of us, however, are the exquisite circumstances from which sound arises, and their connection to our unique relationship with music.

First and foremost, we must understand that sound is an outgrowth of the tremulous, vibratory quality of our world. As we continue to uncover the mysteries of our own physical nature, and that of our surroundings, one of the most prominent revelations is that our world is anything but stagnant. Contrary to perceived appearances, physicists continually remind us what our ancestors have intuited for centuries—that the essence of matter and energy is not fixed, but changeable and fluid. Especially when we consider life at the atomic level, we find the substance of our world to be in constant, bustling motion. So, whether we perceive it or not, our daily lives are spent swimming in a sea of movement and vibration. Things wiggle, tremble and buzz, both inside of us and all around us.

The intriguing aspect of all of this vibratory activity is that it can produce waves or atmospheric disturbances that are projected outward in all directions. It is through these waves that the phenomenon of sound takes shape. Yet, in order for these waves to make a bit of noise, the atmospheric conditions must be right. Sound waves need a pathway, or medium. Molecules need to compress and expand in order for sound to travel.

When we consider the universe as a whole, however, we find these sound-supportive conditions to be exceedingly rare. If we could manage to fly for light years through the vast expanse of space, we wouldn't have the pleasure of hearing a single thing—not our own voice, not passing asteroids, nothing. We would encounter soundlessness because there is no medium through which sound can exist. If, at some point during our stellar travel we were to get homesick for sound, we might have to return to our own solar system in order to enjoy, upon piercing the atmosphere of the Earth, the transformation of crystal silence into spacious sound.

Luckily for us, our Earth happens to be made up of many sound-supportive materials in the form of air molecules, water and other "elastic" substances. When the earth came into being, its atmosphere created a cocoon, or sanctuary; a unique sonorous chamber in the silent boundlessness of space. So, in addition to warmth, light, food and shelter, our beloved Earth provides us with the extraordinary gift of sound.

Still, we know that all the vibrations in the world have little meaning without a receiving device through which to perceive them. And for much of the Earth's history, the humming, buzzing sounds of the environment weren't actually "heard" at all. Even though the Earth probably sounded away with a glorious music of its own, the development of the human ear was a long time coming, evolutionarily speaking, as it was one of the later sensory apparatus to make an appearance. And rightly so, as billions of years of meticulous evolutionary tinkering were necessary to construct this amazing and truly sophisticated piece of elegant machinery.

Yet, it took the arrival of the human animal to bring the perception of sound to a new level, not only through complex and sensitive ears, but also through the development of a large and advanced brain. Suddenly, new light was shed on the experience of sound, beyond the capacity of any species that came before—a vast potentiality that eventually gave rise to the discovery of music. The fact is, when it comes to making sense of music, the ear is only part of the magical equation. Many creatures possess ears, but without the kind of brain that can recognize sonic relationships, music is simply just another murmur in the breeze. Empowered by memory, a vital component in the perception of music, human beings have the unprecedented capacity to perceive an assemblage of incoming sounds as a coherent, whole piece of music.

So, as we reflect on this evolutionary flow of events, we can come to appreciate quite a number of unique developments that had to come about in order for the experience of music to be possible. When we consider how far the human species has come, we might conclude that we are essentially designed to perceive and enjoy music. One of the most fundamental reasons for seeking a meaningful connection with music is simply because we can—if only to fulfill our unique ability, and take fullest advantage of our unique and extraordinary gift.

A GRAND EVOLUTION

Now fully equipped with our keen tools for musical perception, most of us go about the business of our everyday lives, enjoying the energy of music whenever the mood is upon us. As we listen to a string quartet, sing in a choir or learn an instrument, the experience of music makes perfect sense to us. We usually just sink in and revel in the harmonious sound, taking for granted the order, consistency and beauty of it all. What most of us don't realize is what it took to establish the incredibly refined musical enterprise that we are fortunate to enjoy today. Although we rarely consider it, the music of our time has essentially traveled an extended journey to reach our ears. The structures, tools and concepts of music have undergone their own fascinating evolutions, from the picture of early man banging out a rudimentary rhythm, to a full orchestra playing a contemporary concerto.

Imagine, for a moment, how human beings might have learned that through manipulating vibrations, sound could be shaped and organized, creating interesting results. Perhaps forays by inquisitive minds, experimenting with verbal enunciations, transformed the human voice into one of the first musical instruments. New and expressive sounds surely propelled the search for other musical possibilities. At some point some enterprising individual, possibly in striking a taut string, discovered that ordinary sound could expand into tone, and a wonderful new sonic idea came into being. Gradually, higher and lower tones were arranged into patterns, giving rise to the expressive language of melody. After some experimentation, or, more likely, after an accidental confluence, the possibility of harmony was surely revealed when different pitches were played simultaneously. Through the beating of resonant objects, rhythmic concepts began to propel musical ideas with time and tempo.

As human societies burgeoned, the naturally compelling presence of music found its way into cultural fabrics. Each community developed a musical style based on its expressive needs and the materials available in the surrounding natural environment.

Culturally influenced musical concepts, instruments and styles were then passed down through generations, mostly through demonstration and memorization.

Yet, it was around the time of the middle ages in the West that a system of notation considerably advanced the structure of music. Creative individuals who were compelled to express ideas musically, could now inscribe those ideas. Music could now be seen as well as heard, allowing musical ideas to be examined and eventually recorded by others. This development greatly accelerated the evolution of music. Scales were constructed, tested and altered in an ongoing effort to make them sound "right" to the human ear. Reliable systems of tonality were born, providing a foundation for melodic composition. Musical instrument makers tinkered with the physics of sound, improving the variety and quality of musical timbre. And likewise, musicians of all kinds tirelessly developed their craft, elevating the level of what was possible to be performed.

As time progressed, the natural human drive for creation and variety demanded the growth of newer, more expressive forms of harmony, melody and form. Any resistance to change was diminished (though sometimes grudgingly) with each new harmonic invention, allowing for increasing amounts of modulation and dissonance in music. Enticed by expanding opportunities, composers and musicians passionately studied what music could become. Each built upon the musical ideas that came before, much like geographical explorers, seeking fresh possibilities in the newly developing musical landscape. Although tonality had been considerably explored by the onset of the 20th century, the drive to plumb the depths of musical expression did not wane. As a result, exotic musical concepts and configurations continued to unfold. With the advent of technology, music was expanded in ways never before imagined.

So it is clear that everything we know of the contemporary incarnation of music—especially in the West—has come from the work of so many creative minds and spirits, a continual refinement over thousands of years. Therefore, when we listen to a contemporary orchestra in concert, we are witness to nothing less than a revelation, a monument to human creativity and a revolutionary opportunity for power. The modern orchestra with its exquisite array of instruments (melodic tools that have been refined and perfected over centuries) enables the creation of powerfully evocative musical imagery, previously unheard of. And the journey of musical expression pushes onward, and we stand at a very exciting place where the possibilities are only limited to our imagination.

THE CAPTURING OF SOUND

One of the most rewarding experiences a person can have is to be in the presence of a live musical performance. To hear the energy of expressive sound as it is being created – or to be the musician creating that sound—can be a truly magical event. As a matter of fact, right up until the 20th century, live was the only way one could have any experience of music. There were simply no other options available.

Today, the sound of music is a much more common occurrence. We find ourselves constantly exposed to music, both good and bad, often whether we like it or not. And most of the sound emanates from vibrating speakers, rather than actual live performers. This near omnipresence of music reminds us each and every day that we live in an age in which we can capture sound and music in order to have it sound again, often with remarkable qualitative resemblance to the original sound. And once we've made the initial recording, we are afforded the benefit of repeat exposure.

For the greater part of music's history, to hear a piece of music was to listen to it once. Imagine that. Today, we would consider this a musical handicap, knowing how much nuance one can miss with only a single experience with a piece of music. While it is still wonderful to be part of a one-time live performance, the ability to listen repeatedly allows one to become better acquainted with a piece of music, to realize its structure more deeply, therefore enabling a fuller experience.

Access to a variety of music was another limitation of the past. For most of human history, the only experience of music possible for people was the tradition of their immediate culture. Exposure to any alternative forms of music required either the exotic presence of visiting musicians, or actual travel to a distant land. For those relegated to the lower classes, opportunities to hear any music beyond simple folk melody were almost impossible.

Thanks to the marvel of sound recording, we now have access to every type of music imaginable, from fresh, modern compositions to native music from vanishing indigenous peoples. A wider audience is given equal opportunity to expand its sense of musical experience. The egalitarian implications of this development are profound.

In addition to becoming more accessible, recorded music has also become increasingly more portable, allowing us to bring our music with us wherever we go. In this way, we can enjoy music privately, even if in public, adding the dimension of setting to the experience. Sometimes, when I am outside in one of my favorite spots on a beautiful day, I still find myself amazed and appreciative of the privilege of being able to bring a stunning piece of music with me in such a small device—a little performing group in a box. And with digital technology, the sound quality of recorded music is stunningly clear and accurate—an extraordinary evolution from the original gramophone record!

Yet, of course, all things have a loss and gain ratio. The downside of the accessibility of recording technology is how the experience of music becomes ubiquitous, exhausted and cheapened. As modern listeners, we can become desensitized through overexposure. We will talk more about this challenge in upcoming sections. Nonetheless, the next time we encounter a piece of recorded music, we should feel a sense of privilege for the experience, and try not take the fact of it for granted. As we begin a communing practice, it is through mindful, judicious use of recorded music that we are better able to appreciate the opportunity.

♪

In our next section we move on to explore the idea of "power music" and what it can mean for us.

CHAPTER TWO

POWER MUSIC

♭

Physiologically, historically and technologically speaking, this is clearly a fascinating time in which to explore the transformational power of music. And as we discussed in Chapter One, one of the greatest advantages we have is living in an age in which music has developed into a vast and readily accessible art form. In learning to commune with music, a central aspect of our effort involves drawing from this panorama of sound as we build our own special collection of musical recordings. Our selections become essential music—our personal resource of inspiration—and the foundation of our expanding musical perception.

If we stop for a moment to consider the term *music*, we can see that in the 21st century, this word has evolved to include quite a range of time periods and styles. Suggest that we use music in a conscious way in our lives, and we find that we have an awesome variety at our disposal. Where do we begin? Does it matter what music we use in our practice?

Based on my own experience, the answer is unequivocally yes. After much experimentation and discovery, it has become consistently clear that the influence of one piece of music can be vastly different from another. A simple folk melody, a Gregorian chant, a grunge track, a drum circle, an Indian raga, a grand symphony—each of these is created for a different purpose, each has a different experience to offer, and each affects us in a different way.

If we desire to be consciously transformed by the experience of music, the music that we choose to commune with is extremely important. For the purposes of the method put forth in this book, we are interested in communing with music that has power, or what I call *power music*. This term refers to musical expressions that stand apart, mobilizing sound that evokes a significant experience. This is music that humanizes, transforms and enables us to feel more alive.

Moreover, power music is music that we develop a special relationship with over time. Through practices we will learn in this book, we can gain an intimacy that grows and deepens with the stages of our lives. Due to its importance, power music should be approached with focused intention. In a certain sense, this music and what it has the potential to elicit becomes too precious to be experienced in anything other than a conscious fashion. We will learn more about this process as we go along.

For many of us, the idea of approaching music with this degree of dedication and intensity might be an entirely new idea. Nevertheless, our first step is to understand that this type of relationship is possible, and that through practice and experience, we can begin to recognize—and even build a library of—our own personal power music.

A PERSONAL ALLY

Setting out to define just what constitutes power music—what sets it apart from other music—is no easy task. We are immediately shifted into a state of subjectivity, of tastes, where it is slightly awkward and uncomfortable to identify absolutes. Although there are musical sounds that may be almost universally regarded as beautiful, stirring or poignant—Samuel Barber's *Adagio for Strings*, perhaps, or the cool sounds of Miles Davis' horn—ultimately, the perception of power music rests in the ear of the listener. The music we each find deeply appealing is a reflection of the individual person, shaped by culture, experience, and sense of self. Just as we are drawn to particular colors or styles of art, so music beckons the soul in a similar way.

Interestingly enough, there may even be physical clues as to why we respond to certain sounds over others. Peering into the humming and buzzing nature of our universe, it has been observed that objects tend to have a "resonant frequency"—the frequency at which the object most naturally vibrates. When a sound wave of a particular frequency hits an object—or person, for that matter—with the same frequency, the entity will resonate or "hum" in synchrony with the sound. So it may be that when music "speaks" to us, it is made up of sounds that are activating our own resonant frequency—"singing our song" or "striking our chord" so to speak.

♪

Rest assured that there exists a collection of power music that will resonate with each one of us—personally powerful music— the melodies, harmonies and textures of which can uncover a whole new world of experience. Some of us may have already begun gathering the beloved pieces of our power music, whether or not we have considered it this way. It may have started with the first piece of music that captured you by surprise. It is the recording you hold in your hands for an extra moment, with a sort of reverence, before playing it once again.

My own personal collection of power music has developed over the years into quite an eclectic treasure trove that only keeps growing. It includes a fascinating range of material, from my "standards" which are works that have invariably stood the test of time, to current "works in progress"— those pieces whose magic is just beginning to reveal itself to me. And since I have become increasingly receptive to the power of music, I am excited by the prospect of discovering new musical expressions. Frankly, it is hard to hold me back from all the great music I have yet to experience!

However, this is a good point at which to mention that, despite a wealth of choices (just visit any large music store and gaze out over the sea of CDs), I have found truly emotive, evocative music to be quite rare. And as we will discuss, to discover more powerful expressions of music, we may need to venture out beyond our usual scope of experience.

FRUITS OF THE EVOLUTION

The power music I use and suggest is found mostly within the Western tradition. It is what can be termed "art music," consisting of but not limited to classical music, jazz, and other genres, but usually excluding "pop" music. However, genres of music aren't easily pigeonholed. This is a case where language falls short in representing the many varieties and incarnations of music that have surfaced over the years. Nevertheless, we will use the phrase "art music" to refer to music that is created primarily for its own sake as a genuine artistic expression. It is not necessarily music created primarily for marketing purposes or as background.

Due in part to my personal cultural background, I find the range of musical expression afforded in art music to hold the most potential for power. An essential element to this music is the composer. The idea of someone sitting down with the creative mission of writing a composition of music was the next step in music's development from being a more spontaneous and communal experience as was primary for centuries. The impromptu or aurally memorized tradition was certainly powerful and artistic, but it was the arrival of the composer that shifted music into a deliberate art form of amazing potentiality. In many ways, the specialization of composer was necessary in order to discover the extent of what sound could express. Vast emotional power could be poured into and dedicated to the detail of composition. Most references to powerful art music emphasize composers such as Bach, Mozart, Beethoven and others whose music was composed centuries ago. Rarely do we hear of more recent music being held in the same esteem. Yet it is exactly the more recent period of music on which I wish to focus. Overall, I find the most powerful works to have been composed since the late nineteenth century, when music was evolving into newer, more expressive forms.

Yet when most think of contemporary art music, ideas of more atonal, experimental music come to mind—music that may seem more engaging in its analysis then in its actual sound. But what few know is that there is much more. It is true that the composers and musicians of the 20th century effectively tore down the original harmonic structures that had been the foundation of music for centuries. Although some disorder—both musically and socially—ensued, there have also arisen jewels—works whose inventive beauty could only have emerged as a result of the chaos and upheaval of form.

And the story of contemporary music is still being written, which is why I am so interested in upcoming expressions.

All of this is not to say that music which pre-dates the 1900's is inferior in any way. It may simply be that the more recent music to which I refer has the advantage of discoveries which lead to a greater range of expression through sound. In addition, powerful music isn't limited to Western music, or to any particular style for that matter. Any type of music can be power music for an individual. It is only that I have found the spark of beauty in art music to resonate in every aspect of my experience of living. It is this that I wish to share with you.

CHAPTER THREE

MUSIC AND
CONSCIOUSNESS

As we continue our exploration into communing with music, let's be reminded once again that we are regarding music not simply as a means of distracting or entertaining ourselves, but as a path toward enriching our lives by its transcendent beauty. When we learn how to experience it, the power in music can become a vital resource, striking deep chords of inspiration within us. But in what ways can music influence us, and how does this happen?

When we set out to commune with a powerful piece of music, we bring to that experience all the elements of our current state of being—our feelings, moods, and sense of self. As we invite the music inward through the layers and convolutions of our awareness, our communion with the sound begins to elicit various responses. Were we to be examined on the physical level, we might see measureable changes in heart rate, blood pressure, respiration, brain waves, the release of endorphins, galvanic skin responses or "goose bumps," and body temperature. Yet these changes only touch upon the physical, measurable aspects of being. However, what we experience in the musical moment also manifests intangibly, taking the form of insights and perhaps even heightened states of being.

The intensity of these evocations will depend upon the nature of the music and what we bring to it, ranging from the subtle to the transcendent. We can be left feeling refreshed and soothed, or possibly transformed by a powerful communing experience.

Sounds pretty remarkable indeed. But what is it about musical sound—the elements of melody, harmony, rhythm and timbre—that can have such a profound effect on our human consciousness? Returning to those who have gone before us, it is easy to imagine them pondering the same questions, after being deeply moved by a powerful performance. As illustrated previously, science has allowed us to probe more deeply into the physical nature of music and the ways and mechanisms by which we perceive it. These investigations have provided many valuable insights into the physical properties of musical sound, the neurological relationship between music and the brain, and other, more empirical conclusions about how music wields its power.

However, despite these interesting clues into the phenomenon of the effects of music, when it comes to truly knowing why the elements of music can soothe, excite, inspire or enrapture, the answer is ultimately mysterious. It is this enigmatic quality that has given music a mystical aura throughout history, keeping us spellbound to this day. What we do know is that when sound is shaped into expressive musical form, it is somehow able to speak to us in a way that stirs some deep recognition within.

Learning how to commune with this mysterious power not only elevates our own experience, but also the experiences of those around us as we reflect that energy back into the world. We become like amplifiers. In this way, communing with music can truly be a communal experience where we might inspire and motivate others. The following is a discussion of some of the foremost ways our consciousness can be influenced by powerful music. Although they are discussed individually, none of the following effects are mutually exclusive.

REPOSE AND TRANQUILITY

We have all experienced, at one time or another, how our modern lifestyles can challenge our overall sense of well being. We are seemingly always "on the go," often driven by an ever-accelerating daily routine. So many of us are under the added pressure these days to "wear many hats," and wear them successfully. As a result, we may often feel weighed down by stress.

Many of us are looking to find ways to alleviate this modern ailment; methods and practices that can help give us back to ourselves. The power of music can serve this very purpose, as one of the most immediate advantages of music is its ability to have a calming, restorative effect on an agitated mind and body. When we find ourselves feeling the side effects of modern life, the right power music can slow us down, helping to release stress and tension. Settling tempos and soothing harmonies can work to compose our overdrawn selves and to restore a sense of equilibrium.

The theory of entrainment may play a role in the ability of music to relax and calm us. With prolonged exposure to the rhythm and mood of a piece of music, it is believed that we can become "entrained" with it—that is, become synchronized with the pulse and nature of the sound. For example, if we listen to music that features a relaxed tempo and feel, our more active body rhythms can be called into resonance with it, facilitating a change of mood or perception. As we become entrained to the essence of a musical piece, the music can potentially regulate our breathing, slow our brain waves, and stabilize our heart rates. We are left feeling "de-stressed" and renewed. The principle of entrainment works with more lively, energetic music, as well, as will be described in the next section.

This is not to suggest that we have to be stressed out and tense to benefit from the stabilizing effects of music. When in a more equable condition, the same qualities of power music can lead us further into contemplative states. Music essentially creates order out of chaos, as it assembles sounds into organized shapes of style, key and progression, creating an integral, balanced entity unto itself. By communing with the symmetry, harmony, and completeness of musical form, we can be drawn into balance along with it. Moreover, as we discover and gather a solid body of power music, our increasing familiarity with favored compositions can become a place of repose, stability and equanimity.

This effect is enhanced by the technique of "absolute listening," the practice of listening with sustained, open awareness which we will discuss in upcoming sections. The practice of being mindful in each musical moment as it unfolds converts the act of listening into a meditative experience. Achieving this degree of presence, in and of itself, can have a tranquil effect on body and soul. With practice, we can reach supreme states of repose and tranquility—a very peaceful and satisfying place to be.

VITALITY AND INSPIRATION

As human beings we are offered the gift of a dynamic and purposeful existence, but truly understanding and taking advantage of this gift can be more difficult than it sounds. As much as we would all like to live our lives consciously and passionately, at least some of the time, all too often we find ourselves coasting through our existence, often lulled into complacency by the daily grind and the minutiae of daily life. We may find ourselves caught up and distracted from our underlying purpose.

The experience of powerful music can invite a cool, expansive flow of inspiration—like a breath of fresh air. Used wisely and skillfully, the unique experience of power music can wake us up—to revitalize, invigorate, and energize us. Communing with a piece of power music at certain points in our day, even briefly, can serve to reactivate this. It may be the sheer vigor of momentum in a vibrant piece of music that invigorates us, or maybe a more reflective, introspective selection that elevates the spirit. The very act of being fully present with any piece of music that can lead us from our muddled thoughts and concerns to a path of a greater awareness of ourselves and the world around us.

The real glory of a beautiful piece of music is its aforementioned mysteriousness—its almost ethereal quality. It resides outside the realm of our largely self-made or human-made concerns and trivialities. It has no subtext, no agenda. In moments of uncertainty, or amidst feelings of being stuck or blocked, a familiar piece of powerful music can provide clarity, ultimately serving as a reminder of what is meaningful and important in our lives.

Yet whatever music evokes or reminds us of, it is very important to realize that rather than implanting us with something, music uncovers parts of us that are already there. When music inspires or promotes insight or joy, it is only because these impulses are part of our true nature. And in some instances, by uncovering these feelings, it is believed that music is tapping into a wellspring of experiences shared by us all, a truly collective unconscious.

LOVE, COMPASSION AND FORGIVENESS

As human beings, we possess a unique ability to respond to beauty when it reveals itself to us. Over the course of our lives, if we are lucky, we may find ourselves becoming increasingly drawn to beauty of all kinds, catching on that the recognition of beauty can offer some of the most meaningful experiences available to us. When beauty reveals itself through music, however, the sound becomes much more than simply a transient object to admire and move on from. The experience of beautiful sound opens to a much more extensive internal experience.

In lighter, more sanguine expressions, the beauty in music can be pleasurable or comforting to the spirit. But in more intense articulations, the warmth of melodious themes can have a profound humanizing effect upon the soul. When experienced deeply using communing techniques, beautiful sonorities can serve to open the heart of the listener. We may come to the piece feeling rigid and resentful, perhaps subconsciously, yet the music softens our hard edges with tenderness and warmth. At its height, the beauty and tenderness in music becomes a powerful stimulator of our propensity for love, compassion and forgiveness.

Often the seemingly innocent, simple beauty of a stirring melody or harmony becomes more poignant when contrasted with the often complex and unresolved realities of our lives. This juxtaposition can cut through the tight hold we sometimes have on our circumstances, helping us to see more clearly and with greater objectivity into the nature of things. I find this to be one of the most advantageous and worthwhile effects of powerful music. From a clear perspective, the spirit of compassion can move in to enable us to deal with our relationships and circumstances with a greater degree of strength and love—often the only appropriate responses when living in an imperfect, often difficult world. In my experience, compassion and tenderness can sometimes be evoked by the simple yet stunning realization that such intense beauty can exist at all! There are some pieces of music that I personally find so extraordinary, that when I fully experience them, I can't help but be lead to reflect on the workings of the universe as a whole. These works are such precious gifts to humankind, that it is not only difficult for me to imagine life without them, but I also get a sense—a flash—of purpose in a universe capable of creating such beauty.

On certain occasions, when the time is right, an encounter with music can become so exquisite, the expression so exalted, we can encounter peak experiences, similar to the one mentioned in the introduction. The peak experience occurs when the music offers a glimpse of the sacred, evoking an over-whelming sense of wholeness. Tears, or some other release, are a common reaction to this intense state of being, as the music becomes a doorway to the divine. When the opportunity presents itself, these are profoundly spiritual experiences.

Why does powerful music bring forth such a deep inner experience?

In attempting to answer this, it might be helpful to venture beyond traditional explanations. An idea that I favor is that it may be that great music, like all creative genius, flows out of some sort of universal source of wisdom and beauty, inherent in all things. Artists of many backgrounds often speak of the mysterious spontaneity of their inspiration, claiming only to play the role of the vehicle, or channel in their creations. They claim to bear witness to the unveiling of beauty, as though it were already there, often contending to find instead of make a work of art. I, too, have had this experience in my own musical creation.

So it may be that in the relatively rare occasions of creating powerful music, a composer or musician draws from what is sometimes referred to as "the source," the spirit, or the soul. Whatever name is attached to it, it is a source that lies within all of us, within the composers, players, and listeners. In this way, beautiful music becomes a medium for the universe to have expression, revealing itself through us, and therefore leading us back to the truth within.

NURTURANCE AND HEALING

In the course of our lives, each of us will certainly experience times when we are faced with disappointment, loss, tragedy, or illness. The pain and suffering we feel as a result, whether it comes in the form of sorrow, anxiety, or fear, can shake our entire existence to the core and throw us completely out of balance. Although the experience of pain is an inescapable part of any life, the questions become how do we integrate these experiences into our lives and how do we grow as a result?

In our desire to heal, the right power music can become a special source of inspiration, something we can turn to for guidance and strength. When used consciously, rather than as an escape or distraction, the welcoming sonorities of powerful music can have a nurturing effect, inspiring the compassion we need to stimulate the healing process. During particularly difficult times when words tend to lose their usefulness, the unique language of music can communicate in a way that is fresh and spacious. The familiar melodies and harmonies of our power music can serve as a reassuring voice, reminding us of what is ultimately real and important.

As we all may have experienced, our choice of music is important when we are hurting. Especially when feeling weighted down by pain, it is fittest to commune with music that meets us where we are, in some way. Ironically, the one benefit we have in these times is that our pain makes us extremely receptive to the poignancy of beautiful music. Perhaps it's due to the stark vulnerability of distress, but it can almost feel like each note is physically touching us.

If we are feeling blocked or dealing with repressed emotions, the right music can penetrate deeply, acting as a release so emotions may rise to the surface. Within the spaciousness of the musical landscape, and by allowing the waves of sound to give expression to our pain, we are given room to breathe and expand. We can then enable our bodies and souls to heal themselves. This is the most holistic form of healing.

An extended part of the healing process involves using our own experience of pain to connect with the suffering of others. Music's universal ability to touch us all in sorrow and in grief helps us realize that the personal pain we feel is shared by all. In addition, through communing with music we can eventually realize that our experiences of pain and suffering can be our greatest teachers and can ultimately reveal what is truly enriching and important in our lives.

CHAPTER FOUR

MUSIC AND RECEPTIVITY

At this point, it has become clear that the potential of a musical experience is much more expansive than we ever might have imagined. In striving to commune with music, we truly open ourselves to a world of dynamic possibility. And yet there is even more to transcendent encounters with music than what meets the ear; factors that tend to be underexplored, even within music circles. What we find is that no matter how powerful music may be, its influence and effect can be only as resonant as we are open and willing to receive it. In other words, expanding consciousness with music requires more than merely being exposed to it, by, for example, simply attending a concert or casually flipping on the stereo. In order for the sound to penetrate us, for us to be moved and transformed by music, we must be receptive. It is the level of receptivity that is the difference between deeply inspiring musical experiences and those that sparkle with only a fleeting sense of beauty.

If we have been observant we might have already noticed how our reactions to music tend to change under different circumstances and moods. Perhaps we've even noted how the perception of the same piece of music can be different each time we listen. For each of us, there have been memorable times when we felt as though we were being swept away by music, in contrast to times when we felt as if we hardly heard the sounds at all. The differentiating factor in each of these experiences is our level of receptivity. But what exactly does it mean to be receptive in the context of our goal to commune with music? Receptivity involves much more than simply having a musical experience, or being tolerant of a variety of musical styles. To be receptive is to establish a way of being that opens us more fully to the power of music, allowing us to access the wealth of what it has to offer.

On a certain level, strengthening receptivity is about acquiring certain skills: learning how to listen, getting more acquainted with our senses, gaining a sensitivity to musical subtlety, and preparing for communing experiences. Receptivity to music is also contingent upon who we are as individuals and what we bring to each experience. It is aided by our overall receptivity to beauty, subtlety, and joy, and the degree to which we attend to our spirit. It depends upon our ability to open the heart, to learn, to grow—to be open to the mystery of life.

With a bit of curiosity, practice, and experience, we can develop and increase our receptivity to music. Just by reading this far and gently unfolding the many-petaled flower that is music, we have already begun the process. In upcoming sections we will explore many different ideas, practices and techniques, all with the goal of further cultivating the potential for our receptivity.

In this journey we should keep in mind that receptivity is not a destination, or an eventual plateau that we reach and then are through. It is a continual process that evolves throughout our lives. Each experience, each practice, each life lesson increases our receptivity a little more. The wonderful aspect of receptivity is that there is no known apex. We simply don't know the limits of how far we can open ourselves to music, or even how far the communing experience can take us. For this very reason, I still try to find new ways to raise my potential, even though I have gained a substantial degree of receptivity over the years. Whatever our backgrounds as individuals, cultivating receptivity to music can be a gift we each give to ourselves, a way of being that not only enables us to commune with music, but also helps us to become more intuitive with ourselves and the world around us.

9:

So let's begin at the beginning, and start with enhancing our auditory awareness.

CHAPTER FIVE

AUDITORY
AWARENESS

The perception of sound is a perpetual part of our everyday experience. As we are not reasonably able to shut our ears (as we can our eyes), rarely do we encounter a moment when we are not the recipients of some form of sonic material. Yet, even in the face of omnipresent sound, to what extent are we mindful of it? Do we consider ourselves fully acquainted with our sense of hearing, or aware of the influence of the sounds and music to which we are exposed on a daily basis?

If our aim is to grow more receptive to the majesty of music, it is initially helpful to provide a strong foundation through an awareness of sound itself; an investigation into our perception of sound and the many ways it can manifest within our environment. In this section we will discover ideas and practices that encourage the exploration and nurturance of this largely unexplored sensory process.

HEARING AND LISTENING

When sound waves meet and enter our ear canals, the level of awareness involved can certainly vary. We can either hear the sounds, or we can listen to them. As anyone who has worked with the verbal conveyance of information knows quite well, there is a significant difference between the two perceptions. When we are hearing, our awareness is very likely passive, allowing only for a more general reception of sound. By comparison, listening is more active, a willful focusing of awareness to various aspects of our sonic environment.

It is probably safe to say that most of our time is spent hearing the activity around us. We register the traffic, the wind, the refrigerator, the voice of the person next to us on some level—although they are perceived almost unconsciously. This degree of perception is most common in our daily experience, whether through necessity, or simple lack of attention. When our awareness shifts into an active, conscious mode—as though we are "manning" our aural sense, so to speak—we are actually listening to what is going on around us. This is generally rare, and practiced only when the need arises, usually prompted by an awareness of change in our immediate environment or while on the receiving end of some important verbal information. Yet even in these instances when we need to engage our keen sense of hearing, how well do we employ our faculties? Are we even sure what true listening entails?

After a bit of self examination, most of us might find it humbling to admit our lack of proficiency in this area. We might have to "come clean" on our tendency to be "absent" for periods while in conversation, or how we manage to take in whole pieces of music or other auditory information, often with little awareness or retention. Some of us may have to acknowledge never having had the experience of thoroughly enjoying a bird song, or being fully introduced to the unique sound of our own voice! For those of us on the journey toward a better appreciation of the experience of sound, it is essential to know what it is to listen. And, ultimately, if we are to become receptive to music, the practice and ongoing development of our listening skills is elemental, as the quality of our musical experiences is intricately tied to the quality of our listening.

First and foremost, skilled listening involves awareness. We must have the ability to be still and mindful of the present moment. This requires us to stop our endlessly spinning points of attention, and to quiet the mind while centering our awareness upon the nature of the sound at hand. In many ways, thorough listening is a form of meditation. As such, it is a discipline that benefits from regular practice. For many of us, we may be at the very starting point, and will need to learn and practice this skill for the first time in our lives.

TUNING IN TO THE SONIC LANDSCAPE

Despite an abundance of opportunity, it may never have occurred to us to actually listen to the often phenomenal panorama of sound that surrounds us throughout the day. Yet this simple, satisfying practice can be an opportune way to strengthen our listening skills while at the same time cultivating a sharper perception of sound and music.

Following are a variety of exercises that invite us to explore our truly sophisticated auditory capabilities. We can think of

them as a series of ways to become more intimate with the
vibratory energy that surrounds us. In attempting each exercise, we need to practice what I have termed "active listening." This process involves the ability to focus our awareness
exclusively upon the nature of a sound, while at the same time
effectively maneuvering attention among the various sonic en-
tities within our field of perception. We approach active listening first by slowing down, becoming quiet, composed, and
still, if possible. We then try to generate a certain feeling of
contentment, a relaxed and interested attitude toward spend-
ing a few moments in contemplative listening. As we settle in,
we bring our awareness to the present moment, gently letting
go of our current thoughts and concerns. In order to shut out
other sensory information it can be helpful to listen with our
eyes closed, although this is optional. The aim here is to be
simply aware, and to focus our attention on our experience of
sound, without labeling or entertaining any internal dialogue
over what we are sensing. We will be exploring the art of listening in much greater detail in upcoming chapters.

The wonderful and convenient aspect about tuning in to
the world of sound is that we can do it at any moment. The
opportunity to cultivate our receptivity is always at hand.

Exercises

♭ Whenever you find an opportune moment, start by
simply adjusting your awareness to the many
sounds that surround you, allowing them to envelop
you completely.

When outside, take notice of the many layers of
sound—a plane in the distance, a voice down the street,
the whisper of someone next to you—and listen how the
layers of sound can create a symphony of sound colors,
as they weave in and out of the texture of the whole.

After a period, try directing your awareness toward
particular components of the sonic landscape: the rustle
of leaves, various bird songs, a far-off car horn, the lin-
gering of voices, the buzz of insects, a dog bark, the
rumble of industry, the sound of rushing water, the roar
of transportation. Practice shifting your awareness from
one sound to the next, isolating each from the whole, in
turn. Listen wholeheartedly to the nature of each, noticing its particular shape and contour. We can also practice the same exercise when inside, especially within
interesting and varied sonic environments. We can practice pivoting between voices, appliances, machinery and
any other vibrations that meet our ears. While you are
practicing this level of awareness, thoroughly enjoy the
sense of presence that this activity can bring.

♪ Take the opportunity to tune into all the sounds created
by a routine activity—making a pot of coffee, for example. Clear your mind and notice every swoosh and
clunk that arises as a result of the process. Try to notice
the many subtleties that generally fall outside of passive
perception.

♪ Sounds travel to our ears from all directions. Especially
when outside, spend some time registering different

sounds and their location in the soundscape. Without looking, do your best to interpret the distance and depth of particular sounds.

Consider that we can only see the visual field that is directly in front of us, but we can hear 360 degrees! As you focus on one particular sound, adjust your head to various positions. How does your perception change?

♪ Start to notice the role the physical environment plays in shaping various acoustic effects. Compare the influence of a stairwell, a full or empty room, a tunnel, the inside of an automobile, a large auditorium, a deep gorge, a closet, a church, a garage. Listen closely for variations in reverberation, echo, and other acoustic effects. Whenever you walk from inside to outside, take the opportunity to observe the immediate change in spaciousness. That change in itself is a wonderful acoustic trip!

♪ Each vibratory manifestation has a distinct characteristic. Try to discern the different characteristics and influences of the various sounds that meet your ears—a child's laugh, a car alarm, a wind chime, a jackhammer. Which sounds are pleasant? Beautiful? Disturbing? Piercing? Neutral? Interesting? Humorous? When appropriate (and safe), attempt to focus on a sound you find particularly unsettling. Simply try to be aware of the sound, without judging (or cringing). Focus on it until your feel your perception change in some way, or you find something interesting within the sound.

♭ Find a quiet place and tune into the sounds you hear when there is only silence. Spend some time tuning in to that ever-present hiss, and anything else that arises when there is an absence of obvious sound. Try holding your ears closed and focus your awareness on what sounds remain. What is the difference in perception? Are there any new vibrations or sounds? Listen to your breathing, talking and humming; listen intently for any sounds your body makes. After a short while, let go of your ears and immediately sense the change. Take a moment to appreciate how much more dimension our hearing gives us in sensing the world around us.

♭ The vibrations of sound enter us through the skin and bones as well as through the ears. Start to notice the sensation of vibrations as they make contact with the body, especially with lower frequencies. Draw your awareness to the body when in the presence of palpably strong vibrations of sound. Where do the sounds resonate most?

♭ Take the opportunity to listen to the voices of the people around you. Listen to the unique quality of each voice, as well as to the tone and rhythm that support the speaking style of each. Perhaps most importantly, when engaged in conversation, practice making an extra effort to listen to what is being said. Make a habit of giving your full attention to whoever is addressing you. As an experiment, you might try to sustain longer periods of listening without contributing to a conversation, or at least accomplish more listening than talking.

Finally, try to become better acquainted with the
sound of your own voice, the unique essence of each one
of us that can be sensed only audibly. Notice that we
perceive our voices differently than others do, as we hear
ourselves both from within and without. You might even
try recording your own voice in order to perceive the difference yourself.

Auditory Health

Our ability to tune into the sonic landscape is only possible
due to the wide range of perception allowed by our particularly sensitive ears. Yet as exquisite as our ears may be, their
tiny components are far from indestructible, and our hearing
ability may not necessarily be permanent. The most fundamental, and perhaps most important, measure we can take in
promoting our receptivity to sound and music is to properly
nurture the wondrous mechanisms that enable us to perceive
sound and music.

Though the aging process can diminish our sense of hearing, our often high-decibel environments can threaten to ac-
celerate this process considerably. If we think in terms of
thousands of years of human history, this is a relatively recent
concern, which seems to have arrived with the steady industrial and technological advancement of our modern world.

It may be difficult to conceive, but we should remind ourselves that for eons the Earth was a relatively quiet place. We
can imagine how serene and peaceful it might have been, with

only the natural music of the earth to fill the sweet scented air. It was the technological evolution conducted by human beings that brought the current, and clearly unprecedented, dimension of high decibel sound into the world. Although we can point to power music as a welcome addition, much of human noise is not only unwelcome, but potentially harmful.

Just consider a typical modern urban environment. Simply walking through the streets exposes one to an incredible cacophony of traffic, car horns, sirens, voices, car stereos, jackhammers and other construction noise. Even if we try to escape to the suburbs, we often encounter further noise in the form of lawn mowers, leaf blowers and other mechanical clamor! While the sonic landscape of an urban environment may be exciting and vibrant, whether in the workplace, in the home, or on the street, the prolonged exposure to high-decibel noise can pose a serious threat to our hearing and overall health.

𝄢

While we have little control over some of the unhealthful noise we experience, the most serious hazards can be self-induced, through exposure to overly loud music, from car and home stereos, live venues, or through the use of headphones. Headphones become particularly problematic, especially when used for long periods or when the volume is elevated to compensate for other environmental noise. Worse yet, the uninformed listener may become habituated to these higher amplitudes of sound, not realizing that serious harm is being done. Considering all of this, it shouldn't be surprising that noise-induced hearing loss has become a serious concern. And this doesn't even begin to take into account the amount of stress we sustain when exposed consistently to loud noise. The wake-up call comes when we realize that once the inner ear is damaged, we do not yet have the medical expertise necessary to repair it. The harm that is done cannot be undone. This is motivation enough to start paying more attention to the level of sound to which we subject ourselves on a daily basis. We should continually remind ourselves not to take our ability to hear for granted—the precious sense that enables communion with music.

Key Notes

What would happen if we lost even the smallest degree of aural sensitivity? Here are recommendations for keeping your ears performing at their best:

♪ In general, do your best to avoid loud places. If inescapable, do yourself a favor and purchase a pair of ear plugs in order to reduce the level of decibels to which you expose yourself. Of course, be sure to always wear some type of ear protection whenever using loud equipment.

♪ Your home is your place of refuge; be sure to make it as quiet and as peaceful as it can be. A peaceful environment will not only support your overall health, but is most conducive to communing experiences. Take care to be mindful of the volume of computers, stereos, video games, telephones, air conditioners and any other potentially loud appliances or equipment.

♪ Be extremely careful with headphone use and other exposure to amplified music. When using headphones in our communing practice, always keep the volume at the lowest level possible for an effective sound presence. If you cannot hear the person sitting next to you or effectively carry on a conversation while listening, adjust the volume accordingly. Finally, consider wearing earplugs when playing amplified music or attending a particularly loud concert.

♪ Try treating yourself to periodic "silence breaks" during the day in order to explore the pleasures of peace and quiet. If practical, you might even consider a mini, day-long silent retreat. Such an experience can have lasting value beyond the immediate rejuvenation you feel.

"INFORMATION CONTROL"

While unhealthy noise can significantly diminish our receptivity to enriching music, the sheer quantity of stimuli we can be bombarded with on a daily basis is another detriment. Earlier we spoke of the incredible opportunities allowed through the discovery of sound recording technology. The disadvantage of this progress is how recorded sound and other types of media are entwined with the very substance of our daily lives.

We now find music (and the term is used loosely) piped into just about every establishment from shopping malls to government offices. I'll never forget the response I received from a gas station attendant when I asked why there had to be relentless, abnormally loud music playing, even out by the gas pumps. With a shrug of the shoulders he replied, "There's nothing I can do about it. It's broadcast in by satellite." In urban centers, the stimulation can come from virtually every angle, making it increasingly difficult to escape the continuous flow of sound, text and images. We can see television and computer screens everywhere we go—in waiting rooms, in fitness centers, on supermarket checkout lines, even built into minivans.

Yet much of our exposure to media is experienced in the home, as we continue to surround ourselves with increasing numbers of televisions, computers, stereos, video games, cellular phones, home theater systems and palm pilots, just to name a handful. Although the use of these devices can be useful and sometimes necessary, the problem with becoming "plugged in" to this sensory bombardment is that it can take its toll on our inherent sense of peace and clarity. The more we keep stuffing in the sounds and images, the more numb, scattered and overwhelmed we become, often without realizing the cause. Most importantly, an overstimulated, overloaded brain is not receptive to power music.

When it comes time to commune with music, it may be difficult to calm and empty a mind that has received such an abundance of stimulation. It seems the more we require our power music to compete with other music and stimuli, the less room we leave for it to resonate. An important part of becoming receptive to music involves knowing how to create space, to stop the flow of information and to experience at least as much emptiness and silence as we do music. It is only through this contrast that music can become vibrant and meaningful.

Guidelines

Here are some suggestions in gaining a degree of control over the flow of information we encounter every day:

♪ You can start by taking notice of your degree of exposure to the stream of information in your life. Whenever possible, take steps to reduce your audiovisual exposure in any way that you can, at least for a significant period, before communing with music.

♪ Try to break the habit of immediately flipping on the radio when getting into your car, or turning on the television as soon as you get home.

♪ Think twice about playing music in the background for every activity, or wearing a headset or phone as if it were glued to your ears.

♪ Drastically limit your exposure to television in general, and make an effort to participate in computer-related activities only when necessary.

Finally, I suggest you start to incorporate some form of meditation or other contemplative practice as a way to relax and empty the mind on a regular basis. The results of these practices can also motivate us to value and protect a more peaceful and clear state of mind. If our goal is to become receptive to music (and to life itself), taking steps to establish more peace and quiet in our lives is one of the most influential things we can do.

𝄢

The next section will involve shifting gears a bit as we "tune" our awareness to the sonic landscape within music itself and begin an exploration into musical sensitivity.

CHAPTER SIX

DEVELOPING MUSICAL SENSITIVITY

Powerful music has so much to say to us, so much to evoke within us, yet its language consists largely of subtleties. Particularly when speaking of art music, it is through the skillful use of harmonic and textural nuance that a composition can manage to generate such an impressive range of beauty, energy, intensity and feeling. If we are to commune with this wonderful world of aural expressiveness, we must become sensitive to the ways in which music speaks to us. But what do we mean by musical sensitivity?

Having sensitivity to music has less to do with an ability to understand music theory, to identify a theme or style, the possession of musical aptitude, or even the ability to "carry a tune." Rather, it is the unique ability to be responsive to various degrees of musical subtlety—the ability to feel music as well as hear it. We are talking about the capacity to be lifted and carried by the dramatic line of a melody, or to feel a resolution echo deeply within your bones. It is the experience of being swept up by a lively crescendo, caressed by the smooth vibrato of a sustained pitch, or traveling with a driving rhythm. This is a very special trait, one that tends to be rarely seen, even within music circles.

Whatever degree of sensitivity we may personally possess is fundamentally shaped through a combination of genetics and experience. Some are fortunate enough to be born with a certain instinct, an intrinsic vulnerability to sound on many levels. These folks may have a tendency to react intensely and spontaneously to music, often with no prior exposure. On the opposite end of the sensitivity spectrum, there are those who appear to be completely oblivious to music, self-proclaimed "tone deafs" to whom music (and especially art music) "all sounds the same." These individuals can be unmoved by the most impressive composition. Of course, most of us fall somewhere between these extremes. Yet, wherever our aptitude lies, the good news is that a sensitivity to music is something that we can develop and expand.

Interestingly, although musical study and practice can certainly support sensitivity, being a musician or having a musical background is not required, nor does it necessarily confirm a sensitivity to music. Instead, all that is needed is simply a willingness to open ourselves, to become aware, and to gain experience.

𝄢

Before we begin, I must explain that the exploration here is by no means a thorough inquiry into the underlying constructs of music, nor does it include music theory or history. These worthy concepts are simply beyond the scope of this book. What we are concerned with here is the experience of music as it is heard and felt, with the aim of awakening us to the spirit and vitality of musical sound and how it is experienced viscerally.

In order to explore musical sensitivity more effectively, several musical devices will be isolated for individual discussion and perception. At the same time, however, we must realize their interdependency in creating the essence of a piece of music. For the exercises which correspond to these elements, it would be helpful to have a number of examples of power music and a player, although we can also practice the same exercises whenever we encounter music spontaneously in our daily lives. Whenever possible, it is also helpful to have access to a keyboard, guitar or other type of instrument. Lastly, we need not experiment with the suggestions all at once. It is better to practice them over time. As with the practice of tuning in to the sonic landscape, we need to engage in "active listening" in order to properly benefit from the various exercises included here. Yet, since our current objective is to develop musical sensitivity, in addition to shifting our focused awareness throughout the musical landscape, we are also aspiring to feel the influence of sound and notice how it interacts with us.

Finally, we should be clear that actively listening to music is not to be confused with the actual experience of communing with music. The vehicles by which we commune are the "communing techniques" we are to explore in the chapters ahead. The following sensitivity exercises are, like the pursuits in "auditory awareness," effective ways to expand our overall receptivity to music. These are preliminaries and accompaniments to our communing experiences, to be practiced by the seasoned and the beginner alike.

Awakening to Tone

As nature would have it, there are essentially two basic ways that a sound wave can take shape. When a sound is initiated, it sets forth a vibration of either regular or irregular frequency. Each of us should be very familiar with the irregular variety, as it generates the types of sounds that we hear most often— the sounds of footsteps, traffic, slamming doors, ocean waves and other interesting "noises" within our environment. Yet when the frequency of a vibration becomes regular and fixed, it creates quite a different sound indeed. It produces a tone. The voice of tone is pure and pronounced, clearly distinguishing it from other irregularly patterned noise.

Out of the multitude of sounds that nature produces, an occasional tone may organically arise, through a bird song or whistle created by a strong breeze, for example. But generally speaking, it is rare for the natural environment to spontaneously produce the quality of frequency necessary to fashion a tone. It took human beings to eventually cultivate and expand tone so that it could be used to compose a symphony.

Previously, we reflected on the sense of wonder and intrigue our ancestors must have felt by the discovery of tone, and by its ability to be shaped and enhanced under certain conditions. Through persistent experimentation, our investigative predecessors further refined their own vocal cords, musical instruments, tuning forks, and other objects in search of the richest and most resonant tone possible.

Today, we are fortunate enough to reap the rewards of all their efforts, through the beautiful sustain of a Stradivarius or an opera singer's high C. The ability to establish such pure tone also led to a closer inspection into the physical nature of the vibration itself. What was discovered was that a tone can actually be made up of a series of other tones—each sounding together as a unit, establishing the solidity of the overall sound. This series of "overtones" starts with a low "fundamental" or strongest tone, and from there is attended by an ascending pattern of related tones, each sounding with decreasing intensity. Interestingly enough, what this reveals is that a tone is essentially a miniature "chord", even though it is perceived as a single entity. Under normal circumstances, we aren't able to discern these subtle distinctions, but with a little awareness and practice, it is actually possible to hear some of the individual overtones within a single tone. With this many-layered gift of overtones, we can see that there is a bit more to a tone than initially meets the ear. The most fundamental way we can cultivate a sensitivity to music is to awaken to the presence and vitality of tone.

Exercises

Here are some useful techniques to establish a greater awareness of tone in our world:

♭ *Listen for Tones in the Sonic Landscape*—When tuning in to your surroundings, start to distinguish when the environment spontaneously produces tone—the ring of a wine glass, the hum of a motor, the babble of a stream, the honk of a car horn, a bird's song, the squeak of a door. Notice the quality of energy that makes these sounds produce tone and stand out from the other noise of the landscape.

♭ *Feel the Essence of Tone*—If you have access to an instrument, tuning fork or any object that can produce a
tone, set it up in a quiet space. Breathe softly and play
or sound a single note. Listen closely as the resonance of
the tone fills the air. Focus awareness exclusively on the
sound and follow it until it has completely faded away.
Continue, alternating between periods of silence and
sound. Listen for something new in each manifestation.

♭ *Listen for Overtones*—The most practical way you can
listen for overtones is by using your own voice. Sitting
comfortably, take an abdominal breath and sing
the vowel oo with your lips positioned well forward. As
you hold the tone, gradually convert it from
oo to *uh, ee* and other vowel sounds while raising the
back of your tongue. Continue to transition and repeat
the sounds, and try to make the sounds as nasal as
possible. Listen closely for subtle high pitched whistling
and any other interesting tones that begin to accompany
the fundamental tone. Experiment with different mouth
and tongue positions while trying to accentuate the
overtones as much as possible. These vocalizations may
sound a bit funny at first, but with practice,
we can make the overtones more distinguishable.

    Another way to listen for overtones is by getting hold
of a guitar. Sit down with the guitar on your lap with
the neck on your left and locate the D, or third thickest,
string. Play the open string a few times and tune in to
the sound completely. Then take your left index finger
and place it gently upon the surface of the string directly

above the 12th fret. Strike the string while removing your finger a split second after impact. Listen closely for the overtone, which should sound like a partial version of the open string, only an octave higher. It may take a little practice to make the overtone sound clearly. Try the same thing over the 7th fret, where you should hear an A, or a fifth above the D. When you get the hang of it, try other parts of the string while listening for other overtones. Now play the open string once again. Can you hear the subtle overtones within the entire sound?

AWAKENING TO MELODY

A single sustained tone can fill the air with a certain purity of sound, expressive in and of itself. Yet one of the wonderful properties of a melodic instrument is that it is built to convert an initial vibration into faster and slower frequencies, changing the pitch, or the highness or lowness of a tone. We need to take a moment to differentiate pitch from volume, or the loudness or softness of a tone. For example, pitch is the difference between high C, middle C and low C—all of which could be played softly or loudly. The ability to produce a range of tones opens the door to a whole world of expressive sound creation.

When experimenting with different pitches, however, we find that not just any random combination seems to suffice. In order to come up with something interesting out of the immeasurable possibilities available, we have to find a sequence that "sounds good" to our ears. (This is subjective, of course, as was stated earlier. But it gives us a place to begin—a concept we can "wrap our ears around.") The movement from one note to the next must make sense, ultimately forming a complete whole. When we eventually find an interesting pattern, if we are to make it musical, we then need to expand upon it by incorporating such elements as duration, space, and accent. If we are successful, a melody comes to life—the most recognizable and accessible aspect of music.

When we are fortunate enough to extract a great melody from the heap, it can appear perfect and magical, almost as if it couldn't possibly be any other way. What's interesting about a melodic line is that even though it may consist of a series of single tones, it is perceived as a unit. Its essence is created not by any single pitch or duration, but through the relationship formed between these elements.

To change the smallest aspect of a melody is to alter the original idea entirely. Yet there are many ways that a melody can take shape within in a piece of music. Melodies can be built from a number of melodies woven together, be implied within a harmonic progression, or be expanded and developed over the course of a piece. Some melodies can consist of a few captivating notes while others may linger on in evolving themes. Whatever form it takes, the melody becomes the foremost signature of the work.

Despite the fact that the world is overflowing with melodies, truly powerful ones are difficult to come by. When one does arise, it is truly incomparable. Everything about it can feel right and complete, almost as if it is speaking directly to the soul of the listener.

Exercises

Here are some ways to heighten our intimacy with melody:

♭ *Feel the Nature of Melody*—The remarkable thing about melody is that it can express and describe an emotion or idea. With various styles of music, try to identify the melody in whatever form it may take. Sense the melody in its entirety, and attempt to determine its particular nature. Is it sorrowful, bold, graceful, delicate, angular, awkward, smooth, tense, energetic? Is it more ordinary or unique? Is the melody a complete idea, or does it seem to linger without conclusion? As you listen, try to feel its essence. Ask yourself what the melody is expressing. If you were to translate the melody into language, what would it say? What aspect of the melody really speaks to you, or doesn't?

Finally, if the melody is sung and embellished with perceivable lyrics, how do the words affect the overall melodic idea? This is a rather important thing to consider, as what we are seeking here is to become sensitive to pure tonal melody, without the association of words and ideas. This is not to dismiss the use of lyrics by any means, but only to raise awareness of the influence of lyrics on our impression of a piece of music. To what degree do the words influence your impression of the melody? What aspects are you responding to most?

♭ *Feel the Role of Accompaniment*—However possible it is for a melody to stand on its own, most are further defined through the support of some type of accompaniment. The support of a melody serves to establish the ground from which the melody dances and develops. When listening, begin to sense what is the foreground and the background of a musical moment. How does the melody or theme change when placed over different backgrounds? Is the melody accompanied by other melodic lines? Do themes develop and evolve throughout the work? What are the effects of the evolution?

♪ *Learn a Melodic Instrument*—A hands-on way to become familiar with tone and melodic language is to simply try your skill at learning a melodic instrument. A keyboard, recorder, harmonica, dulcimer, guitar, clarinet—the type or sophistication of the instrument is not significant. You might also want to start exploring your singing voice. If you never tried this before, start by singing along with familiar songs or melodies. Try your best to discriminate when you are in tune and out of tune, and if you are up to it, try to build your own melodic lines in the manner indicated above.

♪ *Compose Your Own Melodies*—Sit at a keyboard and play middle C. Taking the sound in fully, hit another key by either a step or a skip. Continue to slowly add other notes in this manner while allowing each about a second of duration. Listen closely to each addition, feeling what works and what doesn't. Keep at it until you compose something that you feel forms a complete idea. After you practice and become familiar with the melodic line, experiment by removing and adding other notes, all the while feeling the subtle changes that come with each revision. What changes make the line more intriguing? What changes detract? If you can manage it, develop the melody by adding different durations and accents in order to make it "sing" as much as possible.

AWAKENING TO HARMONY

Of course, in addition to assembling pitches sequentially, they can be played simultaneously, as well. When we group tones together in a vertical manner, we unleash the potential of harmony—an entirely different and potently expressive means of musical power.

When pitches are sounded together, the unique relationship that is created between them produces an effect that no single tone can match. The sound that arises can be so expressive that it can evoke strong visceral responses within the listener. The remarkable thing about harmony is its ability to convey such a wide range of impressions and images. Each combination of pitches, whether sounded in unison, at intervals, in a triad, or chord radiates a different character all its own.

The terms we use to broadly describe the personalities of harmonic ideas are consonant and dissonant. Consonant harmonies tend to elicit feelings of stability, balance and ease, while dissonant ones tend to elicit the opposite, creating a clashing, unsettling, or unstable effect. Dissonance is restlessness and activity; consonance is rest and fulfillment. If asked, most people would likely be in agreement over what constitutes both consonance and dissonance. (Yet in spite of this probable consensus, these interpretations are still based on listeners' backgrounds and experiences.) In fact, we know that opinions of what constituted dissonant and consonant harmony in Western music have changed dramatically over the centuries. What is considered harmonious to us now might have been considered hurtfully discordant in the past.

To make matters more interesting, we find that these terms are essentially incomplete. To paint a harmonic idea with the broad brush of either consonance or dissonance is to miss the many shades of gray that fall in between the two polarities. As much as we might be familiar with labeling a harmonic idea as happy, sad, bright or dark, there is a whole spectrum of more elaborate configurations that could be described as mysterious, melancholic, exotic, acidic, compassionate, sublime, and a host of other characterizations that are more difficult to describe in words. To my mind, the beauty of more contemporary compositions comes from that they tend to explore the potential of these gray areas to a greater degree, and in the process, come up with some of the most powerful ideas ever invented.

The process of cultivating our musical sensitivity involves becoming increasingly responsive to the influence of harmony—both consonant and dissonant—as harmony is one of music's main vehicles for powerful expression.

Exercises

To expand your awareness of harmony, the following techniques will help you appreciate and cherish the role of harmony.

> ♭ *Sense The Nature of Harmony*—As you tune into the harmonic content of a piece of music, try to experience

the presence of various harmonic ideas. Pay attention to your emotional and visceral responses to each tonal partnership, noticing what "lights up" within you and what doesn't. What combinations are beautiful, plain or coarse? Try to discern the difference between harmonies that are sweet and intense, pleasing and stirring, harsh and stable. What feels like more traditional harmony and what comes across as more exotic?

♭ *Compose Your Own Harmonies*—Sit with a keyboard, guitar or another type of harmonic instrument and try playing random combinations of pitches. Work slowly, starting with one pitch, and then adding a single note at a time. Sustain each harmony for a number of seconds, noticing what each addition brings to the overall harmonic effect. Add and subtract pitches at will, while simply feeling the result of each change. What is consonant? Dissonant? What is neither? Try to compose both the most beautiful and the most dissonant combinations you can create.

THE MUSICAL JOURNEY — TENSION AND RELEASE

From the simplest folk tune to the most grandiose concerto, music is made up of more than just single tones, melodies or harmonies. Music unfolds in time, advancing and developing as it moves along. In virtually any type of music, it is impossible to isolate any individual note, harmony or phrase and still have it represent the essence of the music as a whole. Even though each moment is taken in succession, the essence of a composition comes to life through the sum total of all its moments.

So when we find ourselves responding to a particular sonority, we must understand that our reactions are born out of the context of the whole. It is not an individual moment we react to, but how that musical moment relates to everything that came before. It is through the relationship, once again, between one idea to the next—as with the relationship between notes—that music manages to convey movement, energy and power. In many ways, a piece of music unfolds like a great journey. Along the way there may be many surprises and convolutions, with the possibility of traveling into unfamiliar or unknown territory. The journey may eventually return to its point of origin, or it may wind up someplace new and unexpected. In order to guide the events and stages of the musical journey, each composition tends to establish some sort of a map or framework in the form of key, style and theme that will define the many relationships that are to unfold.

$$\mathbf{9:}$$

Whatever the design, a primary element of music's storytelling process is the interplay of tension and release. The contrast of these two opposing forces enhances music's beauty and expression. The same is probably true in much of life. Depending upon the nature of the piece, the manner in which tension and release plays itself out can vary considerably. The contrast can be mild or dramatic or in constant flux. Release can come in predictable intervals, be intermittent or be delayed by protracted tension. Furthermore, there are a variety of musical devices that can be employed to propel the motion of tension and release. The relationship can be driven by dynamics, changes in texture, or even rhythmic and thematic developments. However, the foremost device used to establish tension and release is the use of harmonic and melodic progression—or the evolution of movement from one note or harmony to the next.

Within the language of harmony, it is the movement between consonance and dissonance that can create a sensation of ebb and flow. Whenever we experience harmonic tension, a certain expectation is instantly created, what we might even consider a gravitational pull, towards release. When dissonance is followed by consonance, and thereby released, we say that it resolves. The intensity of a resolution can vary, ranging from the sensation of simply taking a breath, all the way to the feeling of a triumphant celebratory event.

Whatever the degree, the eventual resolution of dissonance by consonance is certainly the cornerstone of the musical experience. This is the moment where we can rest, and be whole and joyful. The important thing to point out about a resolution brought about by consonance is that its power is entirely defined by the dissonance that proceeds it! Though ostensibly an unsettling idea, dissonance creates the areas of tension that allow consonance to acquire beauty and meaning. Both become necessary parts of the whole.

𝄢

Yet in order for this relationship to be effective, the balance needs to work well. When the degree of either dissonance or consonance begins to outweigh the other, the result can lessen the experience considerably. When music is in perpetual tension, we may find it overwhelming or difficult to receive. Likewise, when music rests in continual stability, without the dynamism of contrast, it can feel prosaic and unchallenging. But ultimately, whatever constitutes the "right" balance of tension and release is something that each listener needs to determine for him or herself. In developing sensitivity, we open ourselves to feel these dimensions within the musical journey.

Exercises

Use these exercises to awaken an awareness of tension and release:

♭ *Sense the Role of Tension and Release*— The moments of our lives seem to unfold in much the same manner as a musical journey. If we are aware, we can clearly sense the movement between tension and release in everyday situations. We can experience this contrast through the process of traveling and returning, working and resting, stretching and releasing, asking and receiving, seeking and finding. Try to take more notice of these many relationships, large and small, and the way in which they form the whole of our lives.

♭ *Travel with the Musical Journey*—When listening to a selection, become responsive to the movement within the journey. Feel the impact of context as one sonority gives way to the next. What does the movement evoke? Playfulness? Intensity? Beauty? Turbulence? Is it indescribable? Perceive the degree of balance between the tension and release that unfolds. Does either the tension or release outweigh the other, or does the relationship work well? How does it feel when there is too much tension? How does it feel when there is an absence of tension? What are the musical devices used to create the effect? Can you detect the presence of a framework that is guiding the journey? What is it?

♭ *Feel Resolutions*—As a harmonic progression evolves, sense its movement. Is it leading somewhere, or does it seem to meander along? Is there a gravitational pull toward some type of resolution? Try to detect when dissonance is resolved and when is it left to linger.

♭ *Develop an Awareness and Appreciation of Dissonance*— It is certainly easier to experience release than tension within the journey, yet we must also generate an acceptance of the dissonance and tension as necessary parts of the whole. Develop a willingness to appreciate proportions of dissonance in music, especially if it means a greater degree of power as a result. With experience, we may even find that some milder forms of dissonance can actually represent another mysterious form of beauty. As a practice, you might try listening to strictly atonal pieces of music without judgment, seeing if you can remain with them long enough to sense something interesting. The acceptance and even appreciation of these dissonant moments in music can help us to be more accepting of them in our own lives.

AWAKENING TO RHYTHM

While the visual arts work with the composition of tangible space, music works with the flow of time. Music works with time to advance the different stages of its journey, paving a type of temporal framework or rhythm as it unfolds. The most fundamental component of this rhythmic framework is the pulse or beat, the most basic frame of reference that orders the timely placement of what is to progress. There may be a good deal occurring simultaneously within a complex piece of music, but it is all held together by the common pulse.

Although it can be sometimes hard to detect, the tempo, or speed of the pulse has a tremendous influence on the overall temperament of a work. A faster tempo can create feelings of excitement, movement and suspense while slower tempos can convey an atmosphere of ease and contemplation, among other sensations. In fact, speeds that run especially close to that of the resting heartbeat are known to have an exceptionally calming effect on listeners. The tempo of a work can be so significant that to alter its speed by only a small degree is to change its character dramatically. We can feel this very keenly when we listen to various rhythmic interpretations of the same composition.

A further organizing feature is that of meter, the use of accents and dividing lines to subdivide beats into smaller, organizational units. Sometimes a specific meter can be felt through the emphasis of a repeating down beat, a reference that marks the beginning and ending of each unit.

Whatever the particular rhythmic framework, each piece of music emphasizes its rhythmic traits in different degrees. Some forms of music, especially percussive, world, jazz and popular music tend to stress beat, accent and meter very strongly, while other forms take a more understated approach. In many forms of art music, it is even common that we find very little semblance of a solid beat or meter at all. Even though a rhythmic framework can be present, phrases may unfold like the cadences of spoken language, or even seem to float about freely.

Key Notes

Consider these suggestions to help you understand the role of rhythm in music:

♭ *Awaken to the Rhythm of Life*—We don't have to look solely to music to get a sense of rhythm and pulse; we can feel it all around us. The steady tick of the clock provides an underlying pulse for many of our activities. We find rhythm within our own bodies through heartbeat, breath and other cycles. We can get the sense of rhythm in our environment through the motion of the industrial and natural world. And if we are really perceptive, we might notice how all the moments of our lives tend to have a tempo all their own. Begin to sense these rhythms and their effects upon your sense of well being.

♭ *Feel the Influence of Tempo*—Different tempos act upon us in different ways. As you direct your awareness to the tempo of a piece of music, try to feel its particular impact. Is it slow, walking, medium, fast, racing? How does the speed of the tempo make you feel? Take notice of any influence the tempo may have on your breathing or heart rate. How do faster and slower tempos affect your sense of time?

♭ *Feel the Rhythmic Character of Music*—Sometimes a single composition can run through a series of rhythmic ideas. Sense when a piece of music is rhythmically consistent and when it incorporates changes in tempo, meter and accent. Feel when melodies and harmonies strictly adhere to a pulse or meter and when they seem to exist independent of rhythmic association.

♪ *Try "Locking In" to a Steady Rhythm*—If it does not already feel natural to you, try to become comfortable moving your body to various rhythmic ideas. When in the presence of particularly strong rhythms, be aware of any impulse you may have to move in sync with it. Do you have the urge to tap your foot or do you feel like you want to move your entire body? Try "locking in" to consistently driving or funky rhythms. Attempt to find the pocket or groove—that spatial relationship between pulse and accent that can be felt in a strong, kinetic way.

AWAKENING TO MUSICAL COLOR

Each musical instrument produces vibrational frequencies in a different manner—through a column of air, via a tight string, by the force of impact, or by electronic means. The particular style in which the individual sound is originated sets forth a specific configuration of overtones. The amount of and relationship between these overtones are what gives rise to its timbre (pronounced "tamber"), or its distinctive sound.

The possibility of timbre adds the dimension of color to a tone or sound—the quality that makes sounds easily distinguishable from other sounds. Fortunately, our brains appear to have no difficulty differentiating between the sound of a cello and an oboe, and with a little experience can even detect more subtle differences like those between a trumpet and a flugel horn. What's interesting about timbre is the extent to which it can influence the spirit and flavor of a musical idea. Even though two different instruments can sound the same pitch, each manages to color that pitch with its own shade, instantly imprinting its own unique personality upon it. For example, a melodic phrase played on the piano will have a completely different effect when played on the flute. The more percussive nature of the piano furnishes each note with a certain attack or "bite," while the more breathy style of the flute establishes a softer and more fluid approach. Although both may be played choosing the exact same pitches, each instrument's sound color delivers the phrase it in its own unique style.

In the same way, the instruments chosen for a composition greatly contribute to what image it presents. Just as pigment allows for different hues of color within a painting, the choice of varying timbres adds more shades into the overall sound texture. Furthermore, the sheer number of timbres can be influential to the experience of a piece. The sound of a full orchestra unveils a powerfully dense texture in contrast to that of a wind quintet. Smaller ensembles tend to promote the individual nuances of instruments or voices more clearly, enabling a greater degree of intimacy with the listener and the means by which the music is created. In developing sensitivity we should begin to take delight in the many magnificent sound colors that are possible within the entire spectrum of music.

Guidelines

Here are some strategies for heightening our sensitivity to musical color:

♭ *Feel the Nature and Nuance of Timbre*—Tune into the various sound complexions of different instruments and voices. What sounds are beautiful, bold, flat or vibrant? What feels fluid, metallic, warm, sharp, fuzzy, breathy, ugly, silky, high, low? Try to indulge in the pure beauty of timbre—the gorgeous sound of a solo piano, the silky resonance of a viola, the angelic delivery of a harp, the heavy crunch of an electric guitar.

♭ *Tune Into the Effect of Musical Texture*—Each alliance of timbres can establish its own unique sound scheme. Feel the textural differences between a wind orchestra, a string quartet, a church choir, a jazz trio. Feel the different degrees of intimacy provided by larger and smaller ensembles.

AWAKENING TO
MUSICAL EXPRESSIVENESS

We know that without musicians and instruments to bring it to life, a composition is simply a bunch of little black dots stretching across a page. The notes have little meaning until they are interpreted and then converted into musical sound. Yet simply sounding the notes, or playing them in any random manner will not produce the music intended. If the aim is to actually create something musical, the way in which the notes are construed and executed makes all the difference.

No matter how simple or complex, a melodic idea must be performed expressively if it is to have any degree of power. If delivered without skill and joy, the most beautifully conceived melody can result in a flat and uninteresting experience. For a comparison, consider for a moment the effect of a monotonous computerized melody from an electric toy to that of the velvety lyricism of a virtuoso violinist. With this example, we can get an idea of the range of interpretation that is possible when it comes to expressing a musical sentiment.

When performing a series of notes, an experienced musician does much more than simply press keys and blow. Through a remarkable synergy of mind and body the musician artfully graces the notes with such subtleties as attack, vibrato, dynamics, legato, phrasing and accent in order to make the notes rise off the page and sing with joy or sorrow, as the case may be. To achieve a truly resonant performance, a musician must also play through the soul—feeling the essence of the music and allowing the instrument to become an extension of the musician's entire being.

Lamentably, many listeners are unaware of the degree of mastery that is involved in being able to play an instrument with such conviction and virtuosity. We are truly indebted to musicians for their extreme dedication and love of the art, as well as their many years of often painstaking hard work that is required to make an instrument truly come to life. It is through their efforts that we are even able to experience the magnificent power of music. In elevating our sensitivity to music we must be able to savor the dimension of the musician.

Key Notes

This is how you can become better attuned to expressiveness in music:

    ♪ *Sense the Level of Soul in a Performance*—When tuning in to a particular interpretation of a piece, awaken yourself to the soul behind the notes. Sense when a musical phrase is played with vitality and warmth, and when it is delivered flatly and without spirit. Feel when a line sings, when it cries, when it laughs, when it whispers, when it shouts, when it screams and when it dances. What is it about the playing that makes the music come alive?

Of course, it isn't any one element explored here that creates power in music. It is through the marvelous cooperation of all of these elements that music sings. All the elements work together to create the essence of a piece of music. In exploring these musical realms, our goal is to venture further and further into subtlety—to become responsive to musical sound at all levels.

As is the case with all the principles in this method, our sensitivity is not something that is a finite destination, but an ongoing development of the awareness of beauty, making us more alive.

𝄢

In the next section we will discuss the seeking and preserving of our own power music.

CHAPTER SEVEN

SEEKING AND PRESERVING YOUR OWN POWER MUSIC

Whether we are seekers who have already amassed a plentiful collection of what feels like power music, or we are neophytes starting out from scratch, the search to build our musical inventory should be an ongoing aspect of our practice of communing with music. When it comes to discovering new musical experiences, there is never really a finite end point to our search.

It could be said that the greater the quantity of beauty we have to draw upon, the greater the range of musical experience we'll gather. This is probably true in all forays into the world of art. Yet, in addition to this resounding aesthetic advantage, the very search for our power music—the process of comparing and contrasting different examples of music which sharpens our musical receptivity—magnifies our musical breadth.

To provide some guidance in this regard, I have appended this book with an exquisite list of works, a compendium that

I have found to encompass an impressive range of musical power. Included in these suggestions is some of my own personal power music. I suggest exploring and communing with a variety of these selections for their strong potential, as well as to provide a reference point and springboard for your own search. However, as we will discuss, searching for and lighting upon a piece of music is only half the story. We must also know how to cultivate and preserve its power so that we may turn to it again and again.

Before we begin, it is worth mentioning that purchasing recorded music might seem an expensive proposition, depending on your budget. Although this may be true in some cases, it is still important to keep in mind our purpose in acquiring our music. Properly chosen, a powerful piece of music can be an excellent investment, providing years of inspiration. Furthermore, we find ourselves with an ever-increasing number of affordable alternatives in obtaining music, making it possible for just about anyone to get involved. Besides, things like these are very difficult to put a price on. The joy and satisfaction that ensues with the finding of each musical discovery is worth the effort alone. The following are some ideas and information to put you on the right track in your search.

POWER INGREDIENTS

Let's start with a question. What makes music powerful and how will I know it when I hear it? As we discussed earlier, no musical device can objectively establish what is felt as powerful and what is not, so this is clearly not an easy question to answer.

We must remember (as I always have to keep reminding myself) that how music is perceived is not, and will never be, universal. The influence and effect of music will always vary from person to person and from experience to experience. That's just the nature of it.

However, one thing we can say for certain is that power in music isn't realized through the study of a work on paper, by its best-selling popularity, or for its impressive technical achievement. Power in music is revealed by how it speaks to the soul. We know the music has power because upon experiencing it, even for the first time, the sound organically touches a place within us, reaching much farther than the ordinary.

The reasons why we may be drawn to a particular piece of music may vary.

For instance, we may be attracted by the specific instrumentation, we may find the melody to be particularly poignant, or we may be intrigued by the creativity of its compositional twists and turns. We may also be stirred by certain climactic moments of a piece—an especially intoxicating lament, the vigorous return of a long-awaited resolution, or simply the skillful execution of the final notes of a phrase. Our hearts may soar over an unexpected chord, the momentum of a masterfully improvised solo, or a surprising juxtaposition of tone colors.

At times, it may be certain composers or styles, or the vitality of favorite musicians that attracts us.

When I search within the tremendous array of art music, I am generally on the lookout for anything that manages to transcend the everyday. Personally, I don't require music to be complicated or even groundbreaking. I look for a sound that expresses its motives in an effective but subtle manner. I usually avoid music that comes across as cliché, synthetic, too cold, "movie sound-trackish" or excessively dark—yet I desire more than sweetness or pleasantness out of music. In my search, I look for music that penetrates a bit further, pieces that employ a deeply affecting balance of dark and light. I have found that it is within this very rare and precious balance that power begins to emerge.

♪·

Despite the fact that I do approach with a certain formula in mind, I always try to be open to the unexpected, taking steps not to judge music by my own preconceived notions. In general, when seeking our power music, it is best to be as open as possible, and not to let any predetermined judgments keep us from discovering something new. We should be willing to—and may need to—search in places outside the comfortable, familiar realm of our musical experience. Keep in mind that as our receptivity increases, our perception of music will become more acute, possibly leading us into interests we never knew we had.

How and Where to Search for Music

Although our modern culture lays a virtual mountain of music before us, we should be prepared for the fact that, on the whole, transcendent music tends to be rare, and most often can be found outside the mainstream. With this in mind, we should be ready to do a bit of investigative work.

I know that when standing in a music store, looking out over the rows and lists of available recordings, one might naturally feel a bit overwhelmed, silently wishing that one's power music might simply jump out of the heap and reveal itself. I wish it were that easy. On the other hand, perhaps we should appreciate the fact that it requires effort, as it is often the search itself that helps us to recognize the precious commodity our power music is when we do find it. Fortunately, we don't have to start without a compass.

The best way to begin is by using the following suggestions and other sources to generate a master list of composers, musicians, ensembles, styles, genres, titles—anything that you feel might be a worthwhile lead.

♪ Spend afternoons browsing the art music sections of music stores, taking your time to get generally acquainted with what is available. Many stores now offer the opportunity to sample selected titles.

♪ Frequent flea markets and other alternative retail locations that feature new and used CD sales. You never know what golden gems you might find.

♪ Make use of your local public library system! Most libraries allow loans from other regional libraries, often providing a wealth of material that you can obtain and investigate at your leisure.

♪ College music libraries often have search engines and listening stations available to the general public. Make use of these often well-stocked musical collections.

♪ Take advantage of Internet web sites that post and sell music. Most major sites even allow you to search for titles and sample your selections.

♭ If you have the hardware capabilities, utilize the Internet in order to download music in the MP3 format, as it is often available without charge or for a significantly reduced price.

♭ Try tuning in to public radio and other programs that feature particular musical styles and genres. Upcoming programs are often listed in the newspaper and on Internet web sites.

♭ Get your hands on a few books, discographies, music guides, current magazines and Internet information for any leads and reviews of interesting recordings.

♭ Put yourself on the mailing list of choice recording companies in order to receive upcoming catalogues.

♭ Frequent concerts, especially ones that feature music with which you are unfamiliar. Look over concert season brochures or check your local listings, as many concerts are free.

♭ Ask fellow "communers" or other music lovers for suggestions, or even start your own musical club to share ideas.

If considering buying a piece of music without hearing it in advance, you can get some indication of what to expect by looking at when the piece was written, the instrumentation and any indication of style and form. Lastly, don't be afraid to take an occasional chance on that hunch, that work that intrigues simply on name and description.

GIVING THE MUSIC TIME

Even after the exciting process of following a lead and obtaining a recording, you still may not know what to expect. Anticipation may be running high and you may wonder whether the music will live up to your expectations. Before setting ourselves up to listen to a work for the first time, we should consider a few things. However possible it is to become genuinely enraptured by a first experience with music (it does happen on occasion), this is not the way it usually works. As impressive as our interpretive abilities may be, a first impression can only give us a partial view of a piece of music. For the most part, it takes a little time to get properly acquainted with the structure, form, context and overall message of a work. Some compositions are especially complex and require a series of experiences in order to be properly digested.

After some first hand experience, we begin to see for ourselves the logic in not putting too much stock in a first impression. We start to understand that becoming familiar with a work is a process, and that our perception of the music will evolve over time. Each encounter with a piece of music reveals a little bit more of what it has to say and if the music speaks to us, over time it may become so familiar that it gets imprinted on our soul. Its movement and spirit will become a part of our own personal cache of meaningful musical power.

As with many forms of creativity in our lives, this process cannot be rushed. There is much more at work here than we might first realize, so it is best to be as patient as possible. For me, some works have taken months or even years to finally "come home." And no matter how many times it happens, I am still utterly fascinated by the process. Yet this deep recognition will not happen with every piece of music to which we open ourselves. And there are those works that will never appeal to us on a powerful level, no matter how many times we experience them.

Whatever the case, the general rule is not to make any quick judgments if we don't respond immediately to a piece of music. We should remain committed beyond the initial moments, and resist the temptation to change the channel, switch the track, or direct our attention to something we think will have more immediate appeal. If, after giving the music a fair chance, you find that the music is still falling short of your expectations, stop listening and put the recording aside for awhile. When the time is right, give it a second chance, taking extra care to be as non-judgmental as possible. If the music still doesn't intrigue in some way, all is not yet lost. At the very least, take note of exactly what elements of the work fall short, and why. By observing in this way, we can treat the experience as an opportunity to heighten our musical sensitivity.

It is helpful to keep in mind that as we progress as individuals, our impressions of our music will grow along with the different stages and circumstances of our lives. In time, we may outgrow a work, or continue to find new meaning in it. Let the process happen naturally and enjoy what it has to reveal about yourself. There's so much music to explore.

MUSIC PRESERVATION

Once a work has consistently risen to a level of stimulation and vitality for us, it can find its rightful place in our personal repository of musical power. However, if we are to preserve the potency of the music for ongoing inspiration, we must learn how to consult it wisely and judiciously. We are developing relationships with these gifts of music, and, as with any relationship willfully and joyfully sought, we do everything in our power to protect its value.

Let's reiterate that power music is music of an especially high caliber—music that we use consciously for self-renewal—so it is important that we only experience it in a purposeful manner, never casually, or as background music. Moreover, when a composition becomes especially meaningful to us, we should give thoughtful consideration to when and under what circumstances we are to commune with it. On the whole, it is best to use our most significant selections only during the most appropriate times, and only when we feel fully receptive.

Just as important is to leave spaces between our communing experiences in order to allow them a certain freshness and vitality. As a general rule, we should always let at least as much silence as music enter our ears.

This degree of restraint may require a bit of discipline, as we all know how naturally tempting it can become to overindulge in experiences that we consider particularly rewarding. Yet too much exposure—even to power music—can leave us overloaded and ultimately less receptive, just as with any other sensory experience. Our goal is to allow our music to maintain the aura of mystery, so that we may gain new insights with each successive experience.

To this end, we should also keep tabs on whatever is "playing" in our heads in between our communing experiences. One of the side effects of developing a sensitivity to music can be an increased tendency to internally latch on to melodies, lyrics, rhythms and harmonies. As a result, we might find our music spontaneously and repeatedly replaying itself in our mind's ear, often without us being fully conscious of it. However persistent and difficult to quell, make a habit of being aware of, and ultimately silencing, this particular imagery.

Lastly, as with any other contemplative discipline, it is important to guard against becoming overly dependent, or even addicted to our musical experiences. We must continually remind ourselves that however meaningful to us, our music is not a panacea, but an ally in our experience of life. If we find ourselves seeking our music as we would a drug, a distraction or an escape, this is a signal to reevaluate our relationship, as well as to reflect upon what it is we are attempting to escape from. Again, it is important that we not rely exclusively on our power music for the development of our well being. It is best used in conjunction with a sound spiritual practice. With proper preservation, our power music can provide years of bliss. It can repeatedly bring us to that spiritual place, like an ally, or a trusted friend.

CHAPTER EIGHT

The Communing
Experience

So far, our exploration has centered around what music is and what it can do, how to seek and preserve our own music, and the various ways we can heighten our receptivity to its power. Yet all of our prior discussion is essentially a preparation and support for the communing experience itself. These communing experiences are the focal point of our work, the moments where we seek to become one with, and therefore be transformed by, musical sound. A powerful communing experience is the culmination of all the efforts of our practice and preparations.

One of the most fortunate aspects of communing with music in our present time is that we can practice just about anytime and in any location we choose. We can commune with music while sitting on a park bench, in a candlelit room, in a parked car, while strolling in public, within nature, with a partner or group, or even in bed before sleep.

However, now is a good time to put forth a reminder of just how different a communing experience can be from what has generally become the norm of listening to music. As we have discussed, inherent in the practice of communing is taking the power of music very seriously, and, with the use of various techniques, experiencing it consciously and purposefully. Yet when we take a look around us, we can see just how far this intensive approach may be from the cultural paradigm we currently follow. Ultra-convenient accessibility, coupled with a mobile, fast-paced lifestyle, has rendered the experience of music more spontaneous and routine. Music has become an increasingly informal pastime, rarely given any special consideration or used for other than casual purposes. As a result, we find the experience of music being pushed further into a background, almost decorative role.

If we take a good look, music has become more of a soundtrack to our activities than anything else. We play music to study to, music to ride the subway to, to drive to, to do housework to, to party to, to dance to, and the list goes on. Rarely, if ever, do we seek music for its own sake, or consider it something we might consciously experience. This passive relationship with music has become so expected that we even see recordings with titles like "work out to the classics," "music for the morning commute," "music to help you sleep." I even remember seeing a compact disc with the title "music to read to"!

A contributing factor to the "soundtrack" usage of music may be the fact that the primary Western (and increasingly global) experience of music tends to be that of the popular or Pop variety. It may be that the more obvious and predictable nature of popular music does simply not encourage anything more than a passive form of listening. Furthermore, it is known that much of piped in background or "mood" music may be specifically designed not to draw any observance from the listener, and designed only to facilitate some sort of amenable atmosphere or enhance the commercial experience. "Music to whet your consumer appetite"—a particularly regrettable incarnation. As a consequence of all these influences, our culture has slowly become accustomed to a more passive, informal relationship with music.

That being said, we move forward, though realizing the influence of these realities. Our new awareness of music will spur our transcendence of what has become the norm. Armed with growing receptivity, we can learn to slowly weave communing experiences into the fabric of our lives. As we begin to see and feel the joy that music brings, our communing experiences can become meaningful opportunities to take time out to celebrate, alone or with others, to be whole, to heal, or simply to relax and be at peace with ourselves.

𝄞

In the next three sections we will focus on "communing techniques," or what to do and how to receive music as it unfolds. Through personal practice and experimentation, I have found these methods to be most effective in bringing one closer to oneness with the essence of musical sound. Each technique has its own approach and style and we start with "absolute listening."

CHAPTER NINE

ABSOLUTE
LISTENING

The expressive sounds of art music can lay quite a bit of sonic information before us, a flowing tapestry of melodic, harmonic, rhythmic and textural relationships. We know that the simple ownership of an ear and a brain is not enough to harness the power of music on their own. Fortunately, we now possess the necessary tools with which to actually perceive these many relationships as they unfold. If we are to be transformed by music, we must know how to put these tools into action—we must know how to listen.

Perhaps we have already gained a degree of experience with conscious listening while experimenting with some of the active listening exercises outlined earlier. Yet the mode of listening we employ when communing with music involves an even more evolved form of awareness. When we are seeking to develop an intimate relationship with musical sound, we are looking for nothing less than the ability to listen with our whole selves—or what I call, "absolute listening." In this principal communing technique we strive not only to sustain a pure form of awareness, but to open ourselves to the sound as well. In other words, we might say that absolute listening involves listening with the heart as well as the mind.

This will be considered our core communing technique in two ways: First, with the understanding that the principles herein form the basis for all other communing techniques; second, with a few exceptions, absolute listening is the method we use when coming in contact with a piece of music for the first time. Becoming skilled in absolute listening provides a solid foundation for our entire communing practice.

THE CHALLENGE OF
PURE AWARENESS

In music as in many aspects of life, the more we give ourselves over to the experience, the richer our experience will be. In absolute listening we give ourselves over by sustained, open awareness of music as it unfolds from moment to moment. Although this may sound simple in theory, it happens to be much more challenging in practice. While the challenge may come in the form of external distractions that interfere with a pure, nonjudgmental awareness of music it is often our very own minds that provide the greatest amount of resistance, hampering our ability to fully absorb the essence of the music with which we are communing. As much as we might like to be quietly present and open to the evolution of a beloved composition, we usually find that a parade of disruptive thoughts and attitudes inevitably accompany the performance.

These subtle intruders can arise in the form of daydreams, random thoughts and concerns, anticipations, comparisons, criticisms and expectations. As our minds indulge in ongoing mental chatter, we find that our awareness of music is significantly compromised. We might even consider all of this mental activity a barrier to our receptivity, a screen that prevents the essence of music from fully entering into our being.

Anyone who has attempted to sit down and meditate has quickly discovered how unruly the mind can be when one tries to focus it on something. Whether attempting to center awareness on the breath, physical sensations or on the spaciousness of mind, one begins to notice how little control one has over the various thoughts and emotions that arise from within. When one observes this first hand, the realization can be a truly eye opening experience. When we sit with the intention of communing with a favored selection of music, we encounter the same challenges as in practicing meditation. For example, as we are right in the middle of an exciting musical development, we might find ourselves suddenly launching into elaborate plans about what we are going to have for dinner that evening, or begin remembering what happened at work earlier that day. We might start daydreaming about that long awaited vacation, or mulling over whatever problems or difficulties we are having at that moment.

As our thoughts continually chime in on our listening, we not only miss the musical moment, our scattered attention gives us only a partial concept of the music as a whole. For this very important reason, it is a good idea to prepare for communing experiences, as we will discuss in upcoming sections. A bit of preparation can aid tremendously in helping to still the mind, especially when we are feeling scattered, preoccupied or foggy.

In addition to mental chatter and distraction, we can face another challenge in establishing a pure form of awareness. As we mentioned earlier, it is our ability to remember that enables us to perceive musical relationships. Our minds have the ability to retain a series of musical moments while simultaneously assembling them into a coherent whole. But our evolving familiarity with a piece of music can sometimes serve as a distraction when we find ourselves anticipating upcoming moments in the musical journey. On the surface, this particular tendency may seem a rather innocuous concern. However, this impulse can become too persistent, continually placing our attention a step ahead. Consequently, our awareness is placed outside of the here and now, the only time where music actually takes shape. The management of this can be challenging, as experience shows us how incredibly hard it is not to anticipate the next phrase, nuance or crescendo. The runaway potential of this impulse tends to negate the musical moment which denies us the full significance of upcoming musical relationships within a piece.

Even if it is the first time we have heard a work, we can still fall into the trap of formulating expectations of what should happen along the way. This usually stems from what appeals to us, or of how we would like the music to sound. This position inevitably leads to subtle judgments and comparisons. When we fall into this rather common critical attitude, we can be blocked from the fullness of what the music has to offer. Paradoxically, a certain amount of anticipation does have a place in the listening experience. As we are taking in a powerful work, there are times when a certain segment can acquire more significance in light of another approaching musical development. Moreover, we know that we find ourselves continually anticipating the future throughout our everyday experience. It is the satisfaction of anticipation that establishes a feeling of security and predictability in our environment. So successfully governing the role of anticipation becomes a matter of balance.

A final challenge or barrier to pure awareness can come from having an analytical approach. In some cases, especially if we are studying music, it is customary to listen more analytically as a method of becoming more familiar with the mechanical and structural aspects of music. There is a time and a place for this type of listening. However, this is not what we are after in absolute listening. Inherent in the process of analyzing is to put oneself in the role of the observer—a purposeful detachment from the experience in order to maintain a certain degree of objectivity. Yet the purpose of communing is not to lean back but to lean into the experience in an effort to become one with the sound.

Clearly, maintaining an open awareness with music can involve a significant degree of effort. As with all contemplative practices, this exertion takes place in the inner world, a silent navigation of subtle fluctuations in the map of the mind.

Although the effort may seem challenging, we should not get disheartened. A certain amount of distraction and resistance is an inevitable part of the communing experience. We simply do our best to be aware of these distractions and through practice, we learn to minimize them, allowing the essence of our music to come through more fully.

GUIDELINES AND THE PRACTICE OF ABSOLUTE LISTENING

Before we go into some guidelines on how to practice absolute listening, we should first understand that there are variety of ways to employ absolute listening. Depending on our circumstances and intentions, we have a bit of flexibility in deciding what degree of awareness we are to apply to our listening. The most concentrated version of absolute listening can involve a pure and exclusive focus on the music itself. This might include finding a peaceful environment, settling into comfortable listening pose, and closing our eyes to allow for a total immersion in the sound.

As an option to this concentrated approach, we can practice with our eyes open while sitting or walking in various interesting environments, or while attending a live concert. Whatever the approach or circumstance, the goal is the same—to establish a high quality of awareness that allows our power music to enter and awaken us.

Key Notes

The following pointers are to be used as a in whatever manner we wish to practice absolute listening.

♭ Spend a few moments creating emptiness by clearing the mind and focusing on the silence or sounds that surround you. After a period, exhale, and start your musical selection. From the first instant the music begins to sound, surrender to it completely, breathing in the initial sound slowly with a full, complete breath.

    With unwavering pure attention, simply be present as each musical moment emerges. If your mind wanders while listening (and it will) be aware of it, and allow each thought or attitude to pass as you gently bring your awareness back to the musical moment.

♪ Whatever arises in the music—consonance, dissonance, the expected or unexpected—accept it and experience it thoroughly. Open your heart to the sound, equally feeling the tension as well as the release. Our goal is not to force a response, but rather to permit the music to move us, letting the music find us instead of us trying to find it. This is not a process of doing but of allowing and letting go.

Breathe firmly and evenly, allowing the abdomen to rise and fall gently. When particularly vibrant musical moments arrive, it can be helpful to respond with our breathing, taking a strong deep breath during a more climactic moment, or exhaling during a moment of release. Most importantly, savor each development. A truly resonant musical moment is a gift. It is within these subtle moments that we become fully alive.

♪ Do your best to avoid analyzing, labeling or searching for a suggestion of meaning. Don't concern yourself with memorizing or acquiring an overall picture of the piece, or even the particular significance of a passing musical idea. This will happen on its own. Listen without naming, comparing, or any internal dialogue whatsoever. Although we may want to experiment with shifting the focus of our awareness around the musical landscape as in "active listening," our aim here is to gather the unified essence of the music, rather than any singular aspect.

♪ Be on the lookout for any judgments or criticisms that may arise, letting them go as you return to an open awareness of the music. Try to manage the impulse to anticipate what is coming next. Let each phrase, each cadence, say what it has to say with no rush. Although we will be working with images and visualizations in our next communing technique, we are not to encourage them in absolute listening. If images spontaneously appear, try to let them go and return your awareness to the musical moment.

♭ Whatever is evoked, allow all responses to flow freely. If you feel the urge to cry, laugh or moan, just let it happen. Feel free to react to the music with facial expressions, or mild movements of the body. There will be a fuller exploration of movement in the upcoming communing technique of "musical kinetics."

♭ If we choose to practice with our eyes open—outside or inside—we can either incorporate what we are seeing and sensing into our experience, or de-emphasize our surroundings, settling into an unfocused gaze. If our environment seems to effectively complement the experience in some way, we can allow what we are sensing to become a part of the overall scenario—the trees, the sunset, the crowd, the smells, the temperature, the entire scene.

♭ If attending a live performance, you may want to experiment with occasionally closing your eyes to avoid becoming distracted by what you are seeing. There may be times when it can be interesting to watch the performers in the act of making music, but we need to guard against becoming distracted by internal comments on the performers themselves. Experiment with this using your own intuition as a guide.

♭ If you are responding well to the music, and find yourself reaching a climax before a particular selection is finished, feel free to fade the music slowly out. It is your option to stop where you are and simply absorb what the music has evoked within you.

♭ Whatever the musical experience brings us, it doesn't have to end when the music stops. As the conclusion of the music delivers you back into the reality of the present moment, remain still, making an extra effort to still the mind. Try not to jump immediately into thought, not even to reflect on what you experienced. Remain in stillness and simply enjoy what has been evoked. Then, after a period, bring your awareness back to your surroundings, taking full advantage of your fresh perspective. Sense your environment anew and incorporate your heightened awareness into the subsequent events of your day.

♭ If, after the experience is over, it was less than you desired, or if it wasn't particularly effective, reflect on what occurred. What went right or wrong? What worked and what didn't? Were you unprepared or distracted? Was the music inappropriate for the circumstance? Were your expectations too high? Use these insights to refine the details of your practice. In general, it may help to understand that the quality of our experiences will certainly vary from one to the next. We can start to accept (and even expect) these natural fluctuations as part of our practice. Our less than satisfactory experiences play a role in creating contrast and ultimately help define what is a powerful experience.

While incorporating these guidelines, keep in mind that there is no set formula to follow. It is through practice, experimentation and patience that we find what works best for us. In the following chapters we are going to build upon the principles of absolute listening in order to explore other ways to commune with music. We move on to "musical imaging."

CHAPTER TEN

MUSICAL IMAGING

Since the majority of our conscious experience is spent interacting with the external world, it is easy to forget that we have access to an internal world as well. When we direct our awareness inward, we find another realm; a field of dreams and images. When we tune in to this inner space, we are offered a different window on reality than that of our usual consciousness.

We all routinely tap into this inner realm, whether or not we are aware of it. Whether through daydreaming or visualizing the past and future, we often find ourselves gazing into space while imagined sights and sounds parade before our mind's eye. In fact, if we pay attention, we might notice that quite a large percentage of our waking hours is spent oscillating in and out of the imaginal world; drifting in and out of memories, reflections, imagined music and sound perceptions, or simply envisioning what is to come.

However common imaginings may be in our overall conscious life, few realize how much influence imaging can have on our sense of health and general well being. Much like our responses to images from the external world, the images we experience internally can stimulate psycho-physical reactions. Through focused awareness, a memory or vision can stimulate adrenaline, cause arousal or excitement, or even produce relaxation. For the majority of us, the unfortunate fact is that we have little control over our indulgence in the imagination, and the resulting effects on the quality of our lives can be profound.

When we spend disproportionate amounts of time in the imagination through excessive rumination, we are simply absent from the present moment, distracted and out of touch with what is going on around us. And when we are full of fearful anticipations or negative images, we are not only distracted, we can make ourselves distressed or even ill. On the positive side, conscious exploration and awareness of the inner resource of imagery can become a means for self discovery and healing.

Motivated by this very insight, the health care community has implemented the use of imagery in past decades to help patients influence things like interactions at the cellular level and postoperative recovery. It is with this very understanding that we explore our next communing technique.

In "musical imaging," we combine imagery with the power of music to unleash a profound vehicle for transformation. One of the reasons this technique can be so effective may have to do with how well music and imagery compliment one another.

It seems that the natures of these two forces enable them to go hand in hand, allowing them to easily coalesce within our conscious awareness. Both can work together as a unit in expanding the potential of the communing experience. And we have a variety of ways we can implement imagery with music.

SPONTANEOUS MUSICAL IMAGING

The first version of musical imaging we will begin exploring is based on a free and uncontrolled approach. In this technique, the aim is to allow imagery to be freely prompted and carried by the wave of expressive music—what I like to call "spontaneous musical imaging." If we haven't already noticed, the many colors of art music can be quite an effective trigger for a variety of internal images. The suggestive nature of the sound can provide a steady stream on which images can float and flow.

Allowing music to shape the imaginal realm can be stimulating and revealing as well. As our dreams continually show us, each of us possesses a rather extensive reserve of imagistic forms within. Many believe that tapping into this wellspring can provide a means of revealing truths about ourselves and our world—a way to access both the personal and collective unconscious.

For this purpose, the use of imagery and music is often utilized by psychotherapists as a therapeutic tool—from promoting relaxation to helping to uncover blocked or repressed emotions. It may be that the combination of imagery and music can open a road inward, a path to our own source of internal wisdom.

Guidelines

These tips will give you a head start with spontaneous musical imaging.

♭ In practicing any form of musical imaging, our choice of music is important. Although we can conjure images with just about any piece of music, what we are looking for here is to incorporate music of a more suggestive nature, sounds that manage to create a musical landscape that is most conducive to imagery.

Determining the exact music for each individual may take some experimentation. Keep in mind the character of a work and what it may call forth. Music of a more adventurous nature will most likely provoke a different type of imagery than music of a more ambient disposition.

♭ A degree of preparation is necessary for this technique, as images are best accessed in a deeper state of relaxed awareness, commonly referred to as the "reverie" state. It is in the reverie state that our brain waves are slowed to the alpha level, enabling a sharper focus on the inner realm. Reaching this state might involve thorough relaxation and settling into a communing pose with eyes closed. The suggestions in Chapter Thirteen (page 123) "Optimizing the Communing Experience," later in this book will assist further.

♭ Immediately before your musical imaging, it is important to spend a few moments clearing the mind, in order to create a canvas on which imagery will appear. Let go of any thoughts centered around results or desired outcomes. Try not to anticipate what is to occur, rather open yourself to the mystery of possibility. We are looking to create an internal wide open space.

♪ From the first instant the music begins to sound, surrender to it completely, breathing in the initial sound slowly with a full, complete breath. As you continue to breathe in the sound, do not force a response, or try too hard to get results. Simply allow the imagery to arise out of the void. When it comes, try not to analyze what you see, simply accept whatever it is.

Inside the experience of musical imaging, we incorporate the principles of absolute listening, balancing our awareness between both the music and the imagery. If we stay in the present, we can allow the music to inspire and develop our imagination. The music is not to serve as background but to give shape and contour to our imagery.

♪ An option in musical imaging is to begin with a certain subject or prompt in mind that can serve as a "seed" or direction for what is to unfold. For example, we might pose an unanswered question to ourselves or bring to mind a current issue or problem into which the music may inspire insight.

♪ Spontaneous musical imaging can be like having an awake dream. As the story unfolds, feel free to explore your inner landscape, trying to involve yourself in your inner scenario. Float or move about, focusing on details such as spatial relationships, colors, surfaces and aromas. Allow the imagery to become as vivid as possible.

♪ At the conclusion of the experience, stay in stillness, allowing the imagery to fade back into the void. After a period, spend a few moments reviewing what occurred. Reflect upon anything significant or revealing that arose as a result of the experience.

♭ If imaging doesn't come as easily as you would like, you can try to encourage it using a variety of stimuli such as photographs, memories, colors, emotions and physical sensations. While in the beginning it may take some time to activate imagery, practice will improve your abilities.

As you explore this technique, keep in mind that each of us can have a unique style of imaging, and there is no "right way" to proceed. It is through practice and experimentation that we can discover what works best for us.

HARMONIZING MUSIC AND IMAGERY

Allowing images to be freely inspired can be an illuminating way to experience a piece of music. We can also use imagery actively and purposefully to explore yet another route to communion with music.

One of the more mysterious qualities of music has always been its inherent elasticity, how its effect and meaning tends not to be fixed, but pliable and resilient. By its very nature, musical sound retains an inherent ambiguity that enables its character and influence to expand and evolve depending on the perceptions and conditions involved. This flexibility allows music to both absorb from and project meaning into the external world.

If we are watchful in our practice, we may become increasingly aware of this phenomenon over time. First, we may begin to notice how our perceptions of an individual piece of music tend to vary under different conditions and moods. Secondly, we might notice how the experience of music can cast a certain aura on whatever we may be perceiving.

We often see this influence of music exploited in motion pictures, where musical soundtracks are added to enhance the dramatic or aesthetic affect of a particular scene. When used well, a musical flourish can accentuate emotional impact. Through association, we may find that a movie's soundtrack has become embedded with the dramatic content of the film itself. When the soundtrack is heard on its own, the music often elicits the feelings exuded by the characters, setting or overall screen story. As we listen it may even be difficult to disassociate the feelings evoked by the soundtrack from the film.

In addition to movie soundtracks, perhaps we have also recognized the influence of music in our own experience; the way music tends to become affiliated with memories, images, or with specific stages in our lives. For example, when listening to music of our youth, the tunes and melodies can bring us back to the places, friends and situations that were part of our youthful experiences. This ability of music to absorb and reflect feeling and meaning provides the foundation for what I call "harmonizing" music and imagery.

This technique differs from spontaneous musical imaging in that the imagery is consciously applied to music rather than allowed to develop freely.

Harmonizing music and imagery involves meditating on an image, thought or feeling while simultaneously receiving a complimentary piece of music. As we focus our awareness on the relationship created between the music and the image, the essence of the two begin to coalesce in our consciousness. Both work together as a unit in evoking our inner spirit.

The benefits of this technique are twofold. The fusion of music and imagery not only can intensify the potency of music, but through repetition, can also establish a certain music/image relationship. Similar to what happens with a movie soundtrack, over time both image and music become infused with the essence of the other. Our imagery can take the shape of visual or other sensory imagery, feelings, or emotions. We can choose to manifest the imagery in a fixed or more fluid form.

EXAMPLES OF MUSICAL IMAGERY

Before we get into some instructions on how to go about this technique, the following are a few examples of imaging ideas, or what I call "imagery programs" that can be used in conjunction with powerful music.

PEAK MEMORY IMAGERY

This type of imagery is based on inspiring memories associated with peak times in our lives. We recall situations, places and moments when we considered ourselves at the height of our abilities. It could be a time when we were in good health, lived with a certain vitality, or when we were in possession of special insights into life itself. As we return to these scenarios in our minds, we revive as many details as possible, attempting to reestablish the energy associated with the specific time and place.

SANCTUARY IMAGERY

These images come from the visualization of our own personal sanctuary within; an oasis that represents our most ideal state and environment. Our sanctuary can be based on real situations or places, or created completely within our imagination. Whatever form our oasis may take, it should be imagined to our perfect liking.

ABSTRACT IMAGERY

This imagery is based on contemplating more abstract states of being such as having compassion, wisdom, forgiveness, peace, kindness, serenity or creativity. As these states are abstract, there can be a variety of ways to manifest images of them. One option might be to imagine breathing in the energy of love, peace or kindness, while another may be sensing the energy arising from deep within. Our imagery could also be shaped metaphorically, as in visualizing a flower opening its petals to represent blossoming creativity. A bit of experimentation may be necessary to find a style that works best for us.

EXTRASENSORY IMAGERY

This kind of imagery consists of images of a metaphysical or transcendent nature. This might involve imagining yourself enveloped in a healing golden light, or flying high above a mountain range. The choices here are only limited to your imagination.

SYMBOLIC IMAGERY

In this form of imagery visualizations are based on a variety of symbols and icons. Here we might draw from our own spiritual beliefs or historical events to manifest particular symbols and representations that are inspirational to us.

GUIDED IMAGERY

During a guided imagery session, a narrative is used to shepherd what imagery is to unfold. This might include following the prompts of a live or recorded voice while listening to a piece of music. The narrative prompts might be based on visualizing the events of an unfolding journey, or outlining a specific state or scenario. We can choose to produce our own recordings, or follow the direction from a live voice.

As we can see from these few examples, we have quite a lot of choices in establishing an imagery program to be harmonized with music. Feel free to draw from these ideas, or even try to design your own unique experience. You can even experiment with harmonizing an imagery program with a few different pieces of music in order to explore different results.

Whatever our intention is—to experiment, to evoke a specific state of being, or simply to accentuate the power of our music—the experience is most effective when imagery and music mutually enhance one another. For example, the act of contemplating compassion may be better suited with a tender adagio than a more vigorous allegro. We should let our musical sensitivity and intuition guide these choices.

Exercises

Follow these steps when harmonizing an imagery program
with a piece of music:

♭ Spend some time formulating an imagery program.
Whether to intensify the music, open the heart, awaken
creativity, or heighten your spiritual essence, decide
how the imagery will take shape using some of the
previously mentioned imagery programs or by developing one of your own.

♭ As with all attempts to manifest internal imagery,
prepare by becoming as relaxed as possible, with the
goal of settling in to the reverie state.

♭ When the music commences, let the sound begin to
stimulate your imagery program.

♭ As you focus, breathe slowly and evenly, allowing the
image and music to establish a relationship. Sense
any particular bond that forms. If your mind starts to
wander, gently bring it back to the flow of the experience. Remember that each of us images in our own
style and it pays to be patient if we find the process
difficult at first. With practice we can discover our
own approach.

♭ At the conclusion of the encounter, allow yourself to be
still and absorb the energy you have created.

When incorporating this technique, be aware that although a single experience can have an effect, it is usually through repetition and consistency that a bond between music and imagery is strengthened. Over time, the imagery and music become permeated with the essence of the other. Eventually we might find that even envisioning the individual music or individual image can produce a particular response. Feel free to experiment with this potentiality.

Using Words as Images

Another valuable asset we have in bringing imagery and music together is to incorporate the use of the spoken word. Whether it be prayer, poetry, affirmations or a story, meaningful prose can unite music and imagery and create a different type of communing technique. The principle here is the same as with harmonizing imagery; we synthesize the words and phrases with music by reciting them to complimentary musical selections.

For material, we can draw from favored words, passages, prayers, quotes, poems or affirmations—any material that you find inspirational, spiritual or meaningful. The strength of this practice comes through repetition. When consistently harmonized, the essence of music and prose increasingly reinforce one another. When we recite along with music, our phrases can be spoken aloud or internally. Reciting out loud has a certain advantage, as our physical enunciation can give more strength and emphasis to the import of the words themselves. Depending on the type of prose we choose, we might choose to repeat a phrase over and over, improvise a bit, or unleash an entire lengthy passage. It is entirely up to us.

As with our other imaging practices, it is important that the meaning behind the words be appropriate for our choice of music. When determining what power music to incorporate, consider length, character and style. For example, a distinct, boisterous movement might not be suitable for a more contemplative prayer. If we choose music that incorporates discernible vocals, consider ahead of time whether or not they could become a potential distraction or conflict.

We may also want to try writing our own recitation or poetry while listening to a dynamic work, having the character of the music inspire the content.

Guidelines

Here are a few guidelines when incorporating the spoken word into a communing experience.

♭ As the music starts, allow a few moments for the sound to set the tone for your recitation. As you begin reciting, feel the music peripherally, letting it fill and support the delivery of your enunciations. Let the phrases be lifted and carried on the waves of sound.

♭ Deliver the stanzas evenly, perhaps in accord with the pace of the music whenever appropriate. Try to find the space where the rhythm of the prose best agrees with the pulse of the music.

♭ As you arrive at a particularly expressive point in the journey, let the delivery of the stanzas reflect that energy. To further heighten the intensity of the moment, vocalize with added tone and conviction.

♩ End the recitation a few moments before the music stops and be still. Spend a few minutes in silence, continuing to soak up the energy of the moment.

Feel free to mix and match techniques; reciting while imaging, reciting before listening, and other combinations. For an added boost we might even consider reciting with a partner or with a group.

HEALING WITH MUSIC AND IMAGERY

As we discussed previously, the elastic nature of music allows it to inject feeling and meaning upon the moments and imagery of our lives. When we are going through especially difficult times, we can use this phenomenon to our advantage and address the parts of us that are in need of growth or healing.

One of the most effective and holistic ways to address our physical or emotional pain is not to run away or escape from it, but to bring it into the light of our awareness. We learn that by truly experiencing the nature of our pain we can then begin to relate to it with compassion and acceptance, an essential aspect of the process of healing.

Whatever the source of our pain, whether it be the prevalence of negative emotions, fear of the future, grief, or physical pain and discomfort, music can create a safe space where we can compassionately confront our suffering.

As we harmonize the image of our fears and distress with compassionate musical sounds, we gather the courage with which to come to terms with our situation, to release our negativity and start the healing process. On a higher level, the experience is not only nurturing but it can awaken an insight into the universality of suffering, leading us to feel deeply connected to all those who are suffering in the same way. Although we may be feeling profound feelings of fear and isolation, the one thing we have going for us during those times is that those states can make us extremely receptive to the poignant sounds of beautiful music. Our vulnerability seems to open a direct channel for powerful music to enter and penetrate us.

Musical imaging can also be utilized to advance the progress of our healing. By harmonizing specific imagery programs, we can take a proactive approach, stimulating our own innate capacity to heal ourselves.

Key Notes

When we find ourselves hurting and wish to include music in the healing process, we can use these helpful suggestions:

♪ Before initiating the process, determine what exactly it is you are trying to accept, heal or come to terms with. We may choose to focus on uncertain aspects of our lives, people to forgive, circumstances to let go of aspects of ourselves to accept, making peace with the past or future, relieving physical pain, releasing hurt feelings, or healing from or coming to terms with illness.

After finding a focus, decide what form your imagery will take. One option is to establish an image by simply being present with, and therefore truly experiencing, the nature of your pain. We also have the option of designing an imagery program that can create a representation of what we are feeling. Use the suggestions from the previously mentioned imagery programs for ideas.

♭ Of all the variations on imaging with music, the choice of music for healing must be chosen with the greatest sensitivity. Our music should be thoroughly suited for our intentions. In my experience, compassionate, tender sounds are most conducive to this purpose.

♭ Whatever approach we choose, we can help the process tremendously by generating trust in our innate ability to heal ourselves. Just prior to listening, bring to mind your anxiety and unease. However difficult, do your best to simply sit and be present with your pain, with a silent determination to simply feel its intensity without struggling against it. As you feel the nature of your fear and uncertainty, allow your heart to become softened and open.

If our fear or anger is extreme, we may want to put off communing to a time when we are in a better position to surrender to our situation. It's important that we utilize this technique only when we feel ready to face in the direction of healing.

♭ When the music begins, allow the waves of sound to fill the image of your hurt and suffering. Stay with the feelings, doing your best to resist the impulse to run or escape.

However sorrowful or bittersweet, the key here is to stay aware and open until you feel your innate wisdom begin to emerge. Allow all responses to flow freely; if tears come, let them further awaken acceptance and compassion within.

♭ In taking a proactive approach to healing, we need to choose an imagery program that will work best with our personal situation. Some options might be to harmonize music with an image of perfect health, sending musically infused healing energy to the parts of us that need it, or even imagining the problem dissolving and floating away with each musical phrase. If we desire to influence physical healing directly, it is helpful to become familiar with the bodily processes in question. This way, we can have a clearer image of what it is we are focusing on.

When practicing this technique with determination, consistency and compassion, we will most certainly see results.

CHAPTER ELEVEN

MUSICAL KINETICS

Although up to this point we have been exploring the various ways that music can inspire movement on the inside, we must not forget that it is also capable of stimulating movement on the outside. The impulse to move our bodies in sync with the pulse and energy of music can be almost as natural as breathing or walking. We need only observe young children in the presence of music to witness this seemingly intrinsic response.

Moreover, we know that nearly every manifestation of human culture has sought to combine the art of movement and music as a means of ritual, celebration or to simply express what it is to be alive. Judging by the sheer variety of movement and dance traditions, it is obvious that there is something very therapeutic and enjoyable about activating our bodies in tandem to music.

In the following communing technique, we seek to build upon this natural relationship between movement and music; a practice I've termed *musical kinetics*. In this technique, the art of movement gives one the opportunity to represent, and therefore "become" the sound in a physical form. By embodying the music, we are led to deeper reaches of communion. Although the concept may be easy enough to grasp, this particular approach to music and movement may deviate somewhat from what most may be generally accustomed to.

Ordinarily, if most Westerners were to envision the idea of moving to music, they might visualize dancing to a steady pulse of the latest popular songs; swaying back and forth, clapping hands, or following a sequence of steps. Yet as our aim here is to personify the energy and colors of art music, there is much more than pulse and vigor that should guide our movements. As we discussed earlier, in addition to rhythm, art music relies on such subtleties as melody, harmony, dynamics, contrast, phrasing and texture in which to convey its message. In order to effectively incarnate the wide range of expression that is delivered by power music, we should be willing to expand our approach a bit. We might need to reach a little deeper, drawing from a range of movements from the most subtle to the overt, the delicate to the more lively.

To get a mental image of what musical kinetics might entail, try to imagine what it might look like to combine the expressiveness of modern dance with the subtlety and fluidity of Tai Chi. It is important to emphasize however, that although visually interesting or even beautiful from the outside, the external aesthetic of our movements should not be the overriding emphasis. Whether a gentle motion of the fingers or a quick rotation of the body, it is more important that our motions be free and uninhibited, taking whatever shape is necessary to illustrate the musical sound. By stimulating energy within, our movements animate the sound while further centering us in the moment.

When planning to practice musical kinetics, we can approach the experience as an improvisation, or we may choose to take a more structured approach by choreographing our movements. With experience we can find the best approach for us. The overall experience should become an expressive, focused and meditative practice.

Guidelines

These suggestions will help to get you into the musical kinetic experience:

♭ In preparing for this technique, we should pay extra attention to establishing a degree of physical flexibility before we begin. Yoga and other stretching exercises can be extremely helpful, not only in loosening our muscles, but for calming our minds as well. Before we start, we should feel at home in our bodies, where movement feels fluid and natural. Loose, comfortable clothing is recommended for maximum flexibility.

♭ Choose a location indoors or outdoors that affords you an unobstructed and level area in which to move about. When practicing outside, a private, natural setting is best. If inside, natural light or a darkened candlelit room can enhance the atmosphere. If you are using a portable player, secure the headset and unit firmly to your body.

♭ Start by getting into a proper stance. Stand with your feet, shoulder-width apart, knees slightly bent. Feel the weight of your body on the bottoms of your feet. Try to find a position where a minimum amount of tension is needed to hold you upright. The most important factor is that your stance be relaxed, allowing you to shift position with a minimum buildup of tension. Stand in place and take a slow, deep breath. Visualize the space around you as a three dimensional plane in which your movements are to take shape.

♭ When the music starts, the objective is to permit the music to inspire the speed, character and intensity of your muscular responses. We are looking for the music to unleash natural, instinctual movements from within—like a banner or flag being filled and shaped by the force of the wind. Especially when we are first starting out, it is best to start slowly and sparsely, by moving a single arm and hand in the space around you. As you gain confidence, gradually include other limbs and movements in the form. Like musical imaging, we incorporate the principles of absolute listening as we allow the music to animate our entire bodies.

It can be helpful to establish some basic guidelines like keeping one foot stationary and anchored at any given time, or shifting one's direction in the shape of a circle. Experiment to find what will work best for you.

♭ Although our arms and hands usually become our main vehicles of expression, feel free to engage all parts of the body; fingers, legs, head, face, waist and torso. Let go and allow your body to become the sound. Try to utilize your entire three-dimensional to express things like melodic line, rhythmic accent, dynamics, chordal textures and various other nuances. The intensity of movement should range from the most delicate gestures of the fingers to the most energetic thrusting of the body. You can choose to incorporate creative ideas like drawing skips and jumps in the air, mimicking the playing of certain instruments, or even envisioning yourself as a wild and eccentric conductor. Whatever the nature of movement, it should be organic, fluid and expressive, flowing outward from within.

♭ While moving with the music, let your breathing flow naturally, responding to the flow of tension and release. Let your breathing aid in your centering or feeling of control. Experiment with eyes open or closed, or a combination of both. Remain as relaxed as possible, avoiding any unnecessary buildup of tension.

♭ As in absolute listening, seize the moment when the music stops. Be still or move gently while staying in the present, fully assimilating the energy that was evoked by the experience.

Keep in mind that the more coordinated and flexible we become, the more command we can gain over our movements. When executed with spirit, the entire practice can become an enlightening and invigorating experience. Feel free to practice with a partner or group.

CHAPTER TWELVE

AUDIO CONSIDERATIONS

It would certainly be ideal if we could have our own personal ensemble, available to play and sing for us whenever we desired. Of course, this will never be an option. Yet, although we won't be able to enjoy the luxury of live music for all of our communing experiences, we can have the next best thing: a digital recording of a live performance. The birth of the digital format has brought the experience of remarkably brilliant and clear sound to the professional and lay person alike—and at an increasingly affordable price. And as the reception of musical sound is central to our communing practice, it is wise to experience music through the best equipment we can manage to get our hands on.

Being in the presence of rich, full, high quality stereo sound can bring our communing experiences to a new level. If we already own some good audio equipment, all the better. If we don't, or we have been listening to music through a squeaky old "box" for years, we should consider upgrading to a system that will give us the best possible sound experience, within our means, of course.

ACOUSTIC PRESENCE

An exploration of acoustic presence is a prerequisite to understanding the specifics about equipment, or the varieties of sonic experience that different audio setups have to offer. Although we may have quite a few options of what type of sound equipment we can use, the manner in which we can experience recorded music breaks down into two basic areas; speakers or headphones.

We can experience airborne sound waves emanating from a speaker cabinet, or we can draw the sound directly into our ears through the use of headphones. Each type provides its own sonic experience. Even though various types of speakers and headphones produce sound in basically the same way, equipment quality, speaker positioning and environmental conditions allow for further variations in the presence and perception of musical sound. For example, on a basic level, listening to a speaker in a room will have a vastly different effect than listening to one placed outdoors. Likewise, experiencing musical sound inside an automobile can provide a different experience than that of a living room or a concert hall.

When speakers are set up within an enclosed space, there are a number of variables that work to determine what degree of presence the sound will create. In addition to equipment quality, the size, materials and surfaces within a room will greatly affect the sound's resonance. For instance when sound waves flow out of a speaker cabinet, they will either be reflected or absorbed by the materials within the room. Ceilings, walls and floors reflect sound while carpets, drapes and furniture absorb sound. If a pair of speakers are to fill a room with quality, stereophonic sound, there needs to be a proper balance between reflective and absorptive substances. Theaters and concert halls are thus designed in order to create the most optimum acoustic environment.

By contrast, the sound you receive when listening through headphones is not affected by these types of external variables. This is why inexpensive headphones tend to deliver a more accurate representation of sound than that of poorly positioned speakers. Yet even within different types of headphones we can find variations in sound presence. Headphones that are placed in, on or over the ears can provide different perceptions of sound. Placed in the ears, headphones can provide greater definition, yet less fullness or bass. Placed on the ears, headphones provide less definition than when in, but can deliver a more balanced range of frequency and tone. Placed over the ears, headphones can succeed in shutting out all environmental noise, providing more clarity and priority.

The use of headphones are unique in that they give the sound a centralized character, adding a certain privacy to the musical experience. With good quality headphones, the music may even seem as if it's originating "in your head." In both choosing and using audio equipment we should become increasingly responsive to these different manifestations of acoustic presence. A sensitivity in this regard will not only enable us to arrange the best scenarios for our communing experiences, but heighten our receptivity as well.

CHOOSING GOOD EQUIPMENT

In deciding to upgrade or add to our communing equipment, there are a variety of options to consider. As a peek inside any electronics outlet will make overwhelmingly clear, our contemporary audio market offers quite an array of "stuff" to choose from: countless varieties of stereo systems, shelves of "boom boxes," multi "surround sound" speaker setups, hoards of digital portable players and headphones, a numbing selection of car stereos, and various multi-format computer-based audio systems. In peering out over all of this, we must first understand that it is certainly not necessary to concern ourselves with all of the devices, gadgets and formats available for creating musical sound. Once again, the sound quality of even lower end modern audio equipment can be surprisingly good, so it isn't necessary to go out and purchase the most expensive gear available. We are interested in equipment that will offer a full, clear stereophonic presence.

Guidelines

Here are some guidelines in choosing the best audio equipment for your communing experiences.

♩ When deciding on a home stereo system, we must consider our needs, as well as where we plan on setting up our system. Today, we have the option of building a system with separate components, or buying an "all-in-one" system that has everything included. The advantage of a smaller, more portable unit is that we can more easily

transfer it to different parts of our living space when desired. Yet while a "boom box" or similar "all in one" system may be less expensive and more convenient, a system
built of independent components and detached speakers
will generally result in a better quality of sound. This is
partly because separated speakers disperse sound
throughout a room more effectively than from a more lo-
calized position. Today, we also have the option of using
our home computer as a stereo system, but this setup can
often be limiting. Whatever you choose, make sure the
system can at least accommodate digital audio.

♪ When seeking to build a system of separate components, the main factor to consider is the device that actually creates the sound: the speaker itself. Even a
mediocre high fidelity system will sound good if it is
driving a pair of dynamic speakers. Our best bet is to
choose quality speakers first, then go about finding a
receiver with sufficient power to drive them to the desired level. Fortunately, this is not generally a hard
thing to do. These days, most receivers will work well
with most varieties of speakers. When checking out different speakers, let your ears be the ultimate judge. The
ideal speaker carries a wide dispersion of sounds in all
frequencies, so that good stereo perspective will be provided through as large an area of the listening room as
possible. Whenever practical, it is best to test speakers
using recordings that feature unprocessed acoustic
instruments rather than processed popular music. Also,
you might consider getting thicker, less resistant wire to
attach to your speakers for optimum sound quality.

♪ Fortunately, choosing a portable player involves a lot less deliberation than that of a home stereo system. I have found the sound quality of even the least expensive of portable CD players to be suitable. When choosing, you might consider a player that accommodates both the CD audio and the MP3 format, as well as a lengthy "skip protection" for minimizing audio dropout. In addition, the quality of headphones you use with a portable unit can make all the difference in the quality of sound presence you receive. If the pair that comes with your unit is unsatisfactory, you might consider upgrading to something that favors a bit more dynamic range. After testing some of the varieties, I have found headphones that rest upon the ear to offer a better sound presence than those inserted within. If you plan on communing with a partner, you can pick up an adapter that enables two headphone inputs at the same time. And remember, be extremely careful of volume level when using headphones in your communing practice.

♪ Whatever room you choose to set up your home stereo system, take some time to experiment with speaker placement. Compare the sound presence that arises when placing speakers on the floor, elevated in book cases, or in other locations within the room. We are looking to find the configuration that will best disperse the stereo sound. When you discover the best arrangement possible, try to locate the "sweet spot"—the position within the room where the resonance and stereo effect will be best felt. As a special arrangement, you might try setting up your speakers 8 to 15 feet apart on the floor and lying down between the two. This particular layout and others can create alternative sound experiences.

♪ Investigate and familiarize yourself with the growing digital audio realm. Involving your computer in your digital audio explorations can expand your options considerably. With access to the Internet you have the option of downloading any music you find onto your computer's hard drive. A digital music organizer and writing CD ROM can give you the ability to "burn" and copy CDs, convert music files into other digital formats such as MP3, as well as allow you to make custom mixes of your own. And, as of this writing, there are new, supposedly more dynamic forms of digital audio becoming available—be on the lookout for these new developments. Enjoy!

CHAPTER THIRTEEN

OPTIMIZING THE COMMUNING EXPERIENCE

A communing technique can be quite an intensive approach to experiencing a piece of music. However challenging in effort and skill, practicing these techniques allows us to commune with, and ultimately be transformed by, musical power. Considering the potential of these musical experiences, it is in our best interest to take a bit of care in what goes into them. If we are interested in getting the most out of communing with music, it is wise to attend to some of the details that surround our encounters.

The following explores a variety of ideas and considerations that can help to optimize each communing experience.

MUSICAL TIMING

In deciding on the best times to commune with our power music, It is worth keeping in mind the following considerations.

Though we may be short on time, it's still important to make time for our practice.

I recommend at least one communing experience a day—but so as to avoid overdoing it we should not exceed four daily episodes. In my own experience, I find that each period of the day presents a different kind of communing opportunity. Communing with the right music in the morning can be an effective way to set the tone for how we relate to the rest of the day. Midday and lunchtime can be a valuable opportunity to refresh and rejuvenate ourselves before returning to our afternoon duties. Communing directly after coming home from work can serve to relax or invigorate us for the remainder of the evening. Each individual needs to find his or her own personal rhythm. Twilight happens to be my favorite time for communing with music. It is a time of slowing down, sunsets, intrigue and new beginnings. Late evening is also promising because of its mysterious nature. This is a good time to be spiritual, to settle down and bring the day to a meaningful close.

In addition to planned or even ritualized experiences, there should always be room for a bit of spontaneity. Although I have established a certain rhythm in my practice over the years, I rarely go anywhere without my portable player, just in case that right communing moment arises. Sometimes the right time to commune with our music is when we find ourselves in a exceptionally receptive state. With experience and increased awareness we begin to feel these states more clearly and therefore are better able to capitalize on them when they happen.

Finally, it should be mentioned that not every time is the right time to commune with music. On those occasions when we feel particularly stressed and distracted, when we are feeling dull, insensitive or drowsy, it might be best to put off the experience to a time when we will be more receptive.

Key Notes

Here are some additional ideas for opportunities to commune with music.

♪ As an alternative to traditional weekend evening recreation, use the time to arrange a special, ceremonial experience.

♪ Plan to commune as a reward for getting your work done, finishing a physical exertion or accomplishing a personal achievement.

♪ Before social events, meetings/gatherings or other occasions, commune with appropriate music to energize, relax or humanize yourself.

♪ Plan communing experiences with a partner or a group. If we have access to like-minded individuals regarding our practice, communing with others can be a unique sharing experience, as well as an opportunity for collective discussion and reflection.

MUSICAL SETTING

Giving consideration to the setting of our communing experiences can make quite a bit of difference in how we receive music. Choosing a setting has a lot to with our choice of communing technique, or whether we planned the experience or are being spontaneous.

When communing at home, a clean, uncluttered, undis-
turbed, comfortable and quiet space is optimum. To facilitate, it may be helpful to shut down any unnecessary
noise-making appliances, computers or air conditioning/heat-
ing units, if practical. We can further enhance the sensory experience with candle light, fragrance or some other special
addition that is meaningful to us. The benefit of practicing inside, in our own space, is that it gives us more control over
our communing environment. We can create a comfortable,
safe, quiet atmosphere while having the privacy to let our
hair down a bit.

᙮

Having said that, some of the most optimum settings can
be outside or in public. There can be few experiences quite
as blissful as venturing out into a natural environment to
commune with music. I have a number of favorite beautiful
spots—natural, green, quiet and spiritual locations that I
frequent on a regular basis. And I also find it intriguing to
commune in more active spots amid the bustle of humanity.
In choosing a location, the most important factor is that
you feel comfortable, safe and uninhibited. Museums, lob-
bies, churches and spiritual centers provide interesting public
settings.

As many of us spend quite a bit of time in our automobiles,
we might wonder whether it is possible to commune with
music while driving on the highway or while sitting in traffic. It
is my contention that when operating an automobile, our
awareness should be focused on driving. And although we can
still enjoy music while we drive, we can give it no more than
passive attention. Therefore I don't generally recommend mak-

ing time in the automobile to commune with music. And an additional note about this: If we spend a considerable amount of time driving, we should consider limiting our music listening to protect against becoming over stimulated and to avoid becoming too accustomed to a passive form of awareness. I suggest varying your driving activities. Instead of habitually flipping on the stereo whenever you get in the car, you might want to take a moment to enjoy the quiet and relative peacefulness that sitting comfortably while driving can bring. I try to avoid excessive rumination by practicing various forms of "driving meditation," listening to various audio books or using the time as an opportunity for awareness practice.

COMMUNING POSE

When planning a more concentrated form of absolute listening or musical imaging, it can be helpful to settle into a "communing pose"—a position that enables awareness without leading to sleep. A communing pose establishes optimum awareness of music by minimizing all other sensory stimulation.

Guidelines

Here are a few suggestions to help you find the right pose for yourself:

- ♭ Sitting in a comfortable chair that supports your lower back, feet flat on the floor while resting your hands on your thighs.

♭ Lying down on the floor or couch with raised head and knees.

♭ Sitting on the floor with your back straight up against a wall, legs outstretched, feet together and resting your hands on your thighs.

♭ Sitting on the floor, or on a cushion on the floor, in a traditional meditation posture.

When deciding which listening pose to use, it may be helpful to consider the style and nature of the music we choose to experience. When experiencing more active or up-tempo music, we may want to vary our position so as to incorporate subtle movements. Feel free to experiment with different positions.

PREPARING FOR MUSIC

Although it may take a little bit of effort and discipline, preparing for music can do much to heighten our receptivity. The idea behind preparation is essentially to "tune ourselves up," a measure to take just prior to the communing experience to become as open and receptive as possible.

Depending on our intentions and circumstances, the length and style of preparation can vary. Our activity can range from a few minutes of relaxation to an elaborate ritual of many stages. This is not to say that preparation is necessary for every encounter with music, or that spontaneity and chance does not play a role in our practice. Whatever we choose, it is simply wise to take a few measures to heighten our receptivity.

Exercises

The following are a few different methods that I have found
to be effective in leading to the most open and receptive state.

♭ Getting physical: Engaging in some form of physical activity before a communing experience can be an excellent
way of boosting receptivity. The stretching and light exertion involved in yoga and other similar practices can work
well to loosen and stimulate our whole bodies, helping to
promote a state of relaxed awareness. Similarly, a brisk
walk, jog or other light aerobic activity can help us to unwind and further settle our bodies before communing.

♭ Relaxation: In our effort to calm down and develop an
inner stillness, we may find it helpful to do some prelimi-
nary relaxation exercises. If we are stressed or agitated,
taking the initiative to relax our bodies and minds can
help us to settle and focus on the communing experience. There are many techniques we can use to promote
relaxation, from the more traditional method of thoroughly tensing and releasing each part of the body in
succession, to simply taking a series of deep abdominal
breaths. Exercises like these can not only help us relax,
but also help us to generate the necessary patience and
stamina to stay with the musical experience.

♭ Clearing the mind: This preparation may be the most
important, since our music is best perceived within an
open and spacious awareness. Taking a few moments
to still and quiet the mind can produce a number of

benefits: First, it can help to clear things out a bit in order to create a proper space for music to enter our being; Second, slowing the mind can help minimize the potential for distracting mental chatter and resistance; Third, establishing a period of silence prior to communing can help create the degree of contrast necessary to give music its well-deserved meaning.

In attempting to clear the mind we might consider traditional meditation techniques—whether focusing on the in and out breath, the sonic landscape around us or upon emptiness itself. Another option is to spend a minute holding our ears closed while meditating on the pure absence of sound. As a general rule, it is best to begin only after we feel that we have created a sufficient space for the music to enter.

Choosing Appropriate Music

When the moment presents itself, we may ask ourselves: what is motivating me to commune with the mysterious power of music? It could be that our spirit is running high and we wish to rejoice, or maybe it is that we are suffering and wish to give comfort to our hearts. We might be yearning for a spiritual experience, or to make contact with beauty. Perhaps we are looking to simply relax, refresh and reinvigorate ourselves.

Whatever our reasons for summoning the power of music, the music we choose is integral to the overall result. The ability to select the appropriate music for different times, states and needs takes a bit of experience. In many ways it can be an art form in itself. When chosen wisely, the right music at the right time can be a revelation, or even a life-changing event. On occasion, it will be very clear what music we should experience and why. We might have a specific imagery program in mind, or we might be planning to relax and unwind. At other times, we might have to give our choice some extra consideration. We start by getting in touch with ourselves and our circumstances. What is our current state of being? Are we stable and content, or off balance in some way? What time of the day is it? What is currently happening?

In choosing from our power music collection, we should select music that best compliments or works with our current situation and state of being. If we are feeling overwhelmed or confused, it is best to choose music that is light and provides a degree of clarity.

When we find ourselves spirited and joyful, particularly rapturous music can accentuate our bliss or even heighten it to a state of ecstasy. Those occasions when we are suffering should be handled with gentle care. The essence of the music we choose must not overwhelm us, but evoke a sense of warmth and compassion.

Other factors like the time of day can be an important consideration as well. Early in the morning and late at night we might consider communing with a more gentle, soothing piece of music. At twilight, we might be interested in more intense music with a celestial flavor.

As we expand our power music collection, we may naturally and informally begin to place each work into various categories—morning music, evening music, music for healing, for relaxation, for a festive mood, for prayer, for inspiration etc. Over time, it will be experience and intuition that guides our musical choices.

MUSICAL DOSAGE

In addition to what music to experience, is how long a communing session should last. Of course, choosing how long to commune first depends on how much actual time we have at our disposal. Are we communing on our lunch break, or are we at home relaxing in the evening?

We must also understand that the length of a work can vary significantly. It is common for musical compositions to be divided into smaller movements or sections, ranging from brief interludes to more lengthy, even epic, passages. In choosing music we must often consider what extent of a work we are going to experience. When considering more extensive works, the degree of sustained awareness that can be required may involve a significant amount of endurance.

Although there are certainly times when it can be a special, invigorating adventure to travel an entire musical journey, we shouldn't feel obligated to do so on every occasion. In my experience, I don't find it necessary or even effective to absorb a work in its entirety if only a specific movement or section works well for me. It is more often that I experience an individual movement or portion in place of the entire composition. To some, the practice of isolating sections of music from the whole may run counter to the original intention of a piece. However, I find that this method works well for the purposes of using music consciously, and there are a few reasons for this.

Music, for all its beauty and grandeur is ultimately a form of aural information that requires a significant amount of awareness and effort to be properly experienced. I have found it to be more effective to fully experience one complete movement, idea or section at a time. In this way, we will not only guard against overloading ourselves with too much musical imagery, but also ensure a sense of closure and completeness to our communing experiences. Furthermore, especially when we are first starting our practice, it is absolutely essential to start slowly, being sure not give ourselves too much to digest in one sitting.

We also have the option of letting the experience itself guide how long we are to continue. I have found it effective to pause or even stop communing if I find myself reaching a particularly heightened peak, if only to allow myself the space to fully experience what the music has helped to evoke. This is something that comes with a degree of practice and experience.

Ultimately, the duration of our musical experiences are less important than their quality. Being fully present with a two-minute movement can be vastly more satisfying than being distracted through an entire symphony. Whatever our preferences, with practice we will gain the ability to obtain more profound experiences in shorter periods of time. When our receptivity is optimal, communing with even a brief composition can transform our entire day.

OPENING OURSELVES

Even though receptivity is elevated by relaxing our bodies and slowing our minds, our preparation is not complete until we strive to open ourselves—to begin with a welcoming, warm and compassionate state of being. As we discussed, music resonates best within a heart that is alive and tender, a heart that is willing to be moved. And the more open we can become, the more we enable the music to uncover our true nature.

Guidelines

These are a few ideas we can use in establishing a more open state of being:

♩ Take a few deep breaths as you let go of your momentary concerns. Generating a feeling of contentment to sit and savor an entire piece of music with the express purpose of living in the present, with nothing to gain but the moment itself.

♩ Take a minute to loosen your grasp on life and give yourself permission to be moved. Take a few deep breaths and envision becoming vulnerable, becoming ready to lean in to the sound. It is also helpful to generate a feeling of trust in the mystery of music. We can believe that our power music has the ability to influence us for the better.

♩ Let go of any expectations that may be brewing in the back of your mind. Neither anticipate what you're about to feel nor worry about whether you are, in fact, going to feel anything at all. Be prepared to be patient and to accept whatever arises as a result of the experience.

♩ Spend some time reading a spiritual or inspirational passage, reciting a prayer or visualizing compassion or other like sentiment. The inspirational content of the writing or contemplation can help stir the necessary parts of us that will enable a sincere contact with the music.

In taking these steps you will be amazed how well they can help you open a space for your music. When incorporating these preparations, remember there is no "right" formula for everyone. Each encounter will provide its own set of conditions to consider. Ultimately, we should keep in mind that the amount of preparation is less important that the quality.

Whatever preparation you do, be sure to fully engage in the process, not as a means to an end, but as an important part of the entire experience.

CONCLUSION

♪

At first glance, *Communing with Music* may appear to be a radical pursuit, a rather intense, aesthetic approach to living. In many ways, it is. However, the use of sound and music in spiritual and healing practices has occurred from the earliest human history. Whether for personal expression or communal rite, we understand music to have held a prominent role in the spiritual and celebratory life of the ancients. The sound of music, when it occurred long ago, must have been a precious event—a retreat from the struggles of that world. It was a time to experience the pure joy of existence.

♪

Although music's integral role in our lives has diminished in recent Western history, attention to the power of music may be undergoing a reawakening. The holistic and alternative health care movements have begun to take notice of the curative energy of music and sound, through music therapy, singing, chanting, drumming and "sound healing." Research in the fields of psychoacoustics and neuroscience has brought new discoveries and greater understanding of the nature of sound and its psychological and physiological impact on us.

Yet, as encouraging as these developments may be, the circles in which their influence may be felt still remain small, and the true transformational power of music continues to be the secret domain of a relatively small number of dedicated seekers. There may be many reasons why this is the case.

For one, very few of us find ourselves fortunate enough to be exposed to music with enough power to evoke any significant experience, so we simply may not be aware that such potential exists at all. Furthermore, vulnerability to an ever-increasing stream of musical and other sensory bombardment may tend to drown out any inherent sensitivity we may have to music in the first place. The ubiquitous flow of information, images and sounds may render the impact of music routine, disposable and ineffective. Finally, even if we somehow discover and attempt to utilize the power of music, our pace of living is still far from conducive to experience such power regularly. Fully realizing this power requires a certain stillness and discipline that our often hectic lifestyles will not allow. Rushing around from one event or task to the next can make it difficult to be receptive to anything, let alone music. And so, the comparatively subtle yet powerful energy of music is at odds with our modern schedules, our noise and our sheer velocity. As a consequence, most remain blind to the transformational power of music, and one of the most fulfilling means of awakening lies untapped. But for those who are attuned, music is a bountiful resource when we learn how to incorporate its wonders into our lives.

Outfitted with the knowledge, guidelines, and practices outlined in this book, I invite you to begin weaving the exquisite power of music into your daily experience. As you set out on your musical journey, keep in mind that the more effort you put into your practice, the more results you will inevitably see.

With patience and commitment, you will eventually reach that joyful moment where, in an instant, you will understand the true transformational power of music, and from then on, as in my own experience, communing with music will be an indispensable part of your life.

Good luck!

POWER MUSIC
SUGGESTIONS

The following is a considerable list of power music suggestions, much of which is comprised of titles from my own personal collection. Most are complete works or parts of complete
works. In some cases, where indicated, several works of the
same style by a single composer are suggested (as with any of
Bruce Stark's works for piano).

With full acknowledgment of the difficulty of placing an
entire musical journey within a single category, I have humbly
organized these great works in order to provide a general
idea of what each has to offer. I have also arranged each list
in each category with what I consider to be the strongest expressions of that category at the top of the list.

The categories are to be considered a rough guide, with the
understanding that none of the listed expressions or feelings
is mutually exclusive. What may evoke compassion and joy
may also lead one to tranquility or ecstasy. While exploring
these powerful pieces of music, we should keep in mind that
most works express or evoke a series of feelings or states over

the course of their journey. Moreover, the way in which they express can vary considerably. Some works convey in a more obvious manner, while others rely on a greater degree of subtlety. Each one of these works has something unique to offer, a powerful experience for you to discover and treasure. Be open to whatever they evoke in you.

Feel free to utilize and adapt each of the works for the various communing techniques, as well as use them as reference points when seeking to expand your own power music collection.

Remember to give the music plenty of time to establish a meaningful relationship.

Happy communing!

COMPASSION AND REDEMPTION

Kernis, Aaron Jay: *Adagio* from String Quartet No.1 (Musica Celestis)

Kernis, Aaron Jay: *Adagio molto* from Double Concerto for Violin and Guitar

Ravel, Maurice: *Adagio assai* from Piano Concerto in G Major

Ravel, Maurice: *Piano Concerto for the Left Hand*

Barber, Samuel: *Adagio for Strings*

Satie, Eric: *Five Nocturnes for Piano*

Yoshimatsu, Takashi: *Requiem from the West* from Symphony No. 2 (At Terra)

Carter, Elliot: *Elegy for String Orchestra*

Corigliano, John: *Voyage for Flute and String Orchestra*

Harrison, Lou: *The Sweetness of Epicurus* from Symphony No. 2 (Elegiac)

Mahler, Gustav: *Sehr langsam* (4th movement, Adagietto) from Symphony No. 5

Bernstein, Leonard: *Symphony No. 2* (The Age of Anxiety)

Diamond, David: *Adagio assai* from Symphony No. 3

Rachmaninoff, Sergei: *Vocalise*

Danielpour, Richard: *Epilogue* from Sonnets to Orpheus

Manno, Robert: *Sextet for Strings*

Vasks, Peteris: *Concerto for Violin and Orchestra*

Stark, Bruce: any of his works for piano

Stark, Bruce: *String Quartet No. 1*

Amram, David: *Hymn* from Cello Concerto (Honor Song for Sitting Bull)

Fine, Irving: *Adagio* from Notturno for Strings and Harp

Satoh, Somei: *Ruika* and *Toward the Night*

Honey, Paul: *Jesus* from the film score, Two Days, Nine Lives

Lauridsen, Morten: O *Magnum Mysterium*

Copland, Aaron: "Corral Nocturne" from Rodeo

Curiale, Joseph: "Forgiveness" from Awakening (Songs of the Earth)

Tavener, John: *Song of the Angel*

Williams, Ralph Vaughan: *Romance for Viola and Piano*

O'Connor, Mark: *Vistas* and *Poem for Carlita*

Oldham, Kevin: *Andante tranquillo* from Concerto for Piano

Douglas, Roy: *Cantilena*

Hindemith, Paul: *Ludus Tonalis*

Metheny, Pat: *A Map of the World* (music from and inspired by the motion picture)

Rózsa, Miklós: *Allegro non trappo* from Concerto for Violin and Orchestra

Rózsa, Miklós: *Lento* from Concerto for Violin and Orchestra

Persichetti, Vincent: *Hollow Men*

LOVE AND WARMTH

Danielpour, Richard: *In Paradisum* (Élégies)

Ravel, Maurice: *String Quartet in F Major*

Ravel, Maurice: *Pavane Pour Une Infante Défunte*

Williams, Ralph Vaughan: *The Lark Ascending*

Williams, Ralph Vaughan: *Concerto for Violin and Orchestra*

Canning, Thomas: *Fantasy on a Hymn Tune by Justin Morgan*

Kernis, Aaron Jay: *Air for Violin and Orchestra*

Foss, Lukas: *Three American Pieces*

Webern, Anton: *Langsamer satz* (slow movement) for String Quartet

Delius, Frederick: *On Hearing the First Cuckoo in Spring*

Delius, Frederick: *Air and Dance*

Copland, Aaron: *Appalachian Spring*

Copland, Aaron: *Our Town*

Stravinsky, Igor: *Variation d'Apollon, Pas de Deux*, and *Coda from Apollon Musagète*

Villa-Lobos, Heitor: *String Quartets Nos. 8, 13 and 14*

Mozetich, Marjan: *Affairs of the Heart* and *Postcards from the Sky*

Diamond, David: *Andante semplice* and *Adagio sospirando* from Romeo and Juliet

Beaser, Robert: *Psalm 119*

Barber, Samuel: *Adagio* from Cello Concerto in A Minor

Barber, Samuel: *The School for Scandal*

Barber, Samuel: *Knoxville: Summer of 1915*

Kabalevsky, Dmitry: any of his works for piano

Borodin, Alexander: String Quartet No. 1

Rorem, Ned: *Berceuse* (Lullaby) from String Symphony

Rorem, Ned: *Romance Without Words* and *Midnight* from Violin Concerto

Elgar, Edward: *Nimrod* from Enigma Variations

Elgar, Edward: *Sospiri*

Hanson, Howard: *Love Duet* from Merry Mount Suite

Hanson, Howard: *Concerto for Piano*

Finzi, Gerald: *Concerto for Clarinet and String Orchestra in C Minor, 2nd movement*

Debussy, Claude: *Twelve Études for Piano, pieces 4, 8 and 11*

Debussy, Claude: Prélude à l'après-midi d'un faune (Prelude to the Afternoon of a Faun)

Bartók, Béla: Adagio religioso from Piano Concerto No. 3

Britten, Benjamin: Let Us Sleep Now from War Requiem

Tailleferre, Germaine: Ballad for Piano and Orchestra

Wood, Haydn: Andante from Fantasy Concerto

Warlock, Peter: *Serenade to Frederick Delius on His 60th Birthday*

Chávez, Carlos: Suite for Double Quartet

Bruch, Max: *Violin Concerto No.1*

Bridge, Frank: *Sally in Our Alley*

Creston, Paul: *Cantilena* from Choreografic Suite, Op. 86a

Koechlin, Charles: *Au Loin*, Piece Symphonique

Reade, Paul: *Mists* from Victorian Kitchen Garden

Foss, Lukas: *Romance*

Poulenc, Francis: *Sonata for Oboe and Piano*

Previn, Andre: *Honey and Rue*

Yoshimatsu, Takashi: *Water* and *Air* from Symphony No. 1

JOY AND ECSTASY

Picker, Tobias: *Old and Lost Rivers*

Copland, Aaron: *Clarinet Concerto*

Copland, Aaron: *Quiet City*

Copland, Aaron: *Dance Panels*

Mahler, Gustav: *Symphony No. 9*

Guy, Barry: *After the Rain*

Bernstein, Leonard: *Clarinet Concerto*

Górecki, Henryk: *Symphony No. 3*

Corea, Chick: *Piano Concerto*

Ravel, Maurice: *Le Jardin Feerique* from Ma Mère L'Oye

Ravel, Maurice: *Interlude* from Daphnis et Chloe

Hovhaness, Alan: *Andante* from Symphony No. 2 (Mysterious Mountain)

Britten, Benjamin: *Sinfonietta*

Yoshimatsu, Takashi: *Guitar Concerto* (Pegasus Effect)

Yoshimatsu, Takashi: *And Birds are Still*, Op. 72

Korngold, Erich Wolfgang: *Theme and Variations*

Korngold, Erich Wolfgang: *Violin Concerto in D Major*

Vasks, Peteris: *Cantabile*

Hancock, Herbie: *Lullaby* from the album, Gershwin's World

Williams, Ralph Vaughan: *Concerto for Oboe and String Orchestra in A Minor*

Debussy, Claude: *La Cathédrale Engloutie*

Respighi, Ottorino: *The Pines of Rome*

Walton, William: *Touch Her Soft Lips and Part* from *Henry V* film score

Manno, Robert: *Three Poems*

Piston, Walter: *Adagio* from Symphony No. 6 (Gettysburg)

Piston, Walter: *Adagio* from Concerto for Violin and Orchestra

Schuman, William: *Adagio* from New England Triptych

Amram, David: *Blues* from American Dance Suite

Amram, David: *Theme and Variations on Red River Valley*

Kernis, Aaron Jay: *String Quartet No. 2*

Bernstein, Leonard: *Agathon* from Serenade

Honegger, Arthur: *Pacific 231*

Larson, Libby: *Elegance* and *Beauty Alone* from Symphony No. 4 (String Symphony)

Henze, Hans Werner: *Adagio, Adagio, Serenade*

Drescher, Paul: *Night Songs*

Childs, Billy: *The Distant Land*

LONGING AND SORROW

Puccini, Giacomo: *Crisantemi*

Barber, Samuel: *Essays for Orchestra*

Barber, Samuel: *Andante* from Violin Concerto

Barber, Samuel: *Andante tranquillo* from Symphony No. 1

Diamond, David: *Adagio* from Symphony No. 11

Debussy, Claude: *String Quartet*

Satie, Erik: *Six Gnossiennes*

Schoenberg, Arnold: *Verklärte Nacht*

Atterberg, Kurt: *Suite for Violin, Viola and Orchestra*

Walton, William: *Passacagila* from *Henry V* film score

Koechlin, Charles: *Sur Le Flots Lointains*, Op. 130

Van Beethoven, Ludwig: *Cavatina* from String Quartet No. 13, Op. 130

Szymanowski, Karol: any of his works for violin and piano

Williams, Ralph Vaughan: *Concerto Grosso for Strings*

Drescher, Paul: *Double Ikat*

Korngold, Erich Wolfgang: *Suite for 2 Violins, Cello and Piano* (Left Hand), 2nd and 4th movements

Fine, Irving: *Serious Song* (Lament for String Orchestra)

Hersch, Fred: *Tango Bittersweet*

Messiaen, Olivier: *Eulogy to the Eternity of Jesus* from Quartet for the End of Time

Herrmann, Bernard: Farenheit 451, film score

Korngold, Erich Wolfgang: *Symphony in F sharp*

Fauré, Gabriel: *Élégie for Cello and Piano*, Op. 24

Bernstein, Leonard: *Lamentation* from Symphony No. 1 (Jeremiah)

Grieg, Edvard: *Heimweh* (Homesickness)

Miaskovsky, Nikolay: *Cello Concerto in C Minor*

Williams, John: *Angela's Ashes*, film score

Corigliano, John: *The Red Violin*, film score

Schmidt, Franz: *Quintet for Piano* (Left Hand) and *String Quartet in G Major*

Liszt, Franz: *Consolation No. 3 in D flat Major*

Chopin, Frédéric: *Etude in C sharp Minor*, Op. 25

Chopin, Frédéric: *Nocturne in D flat*, Op. 27

Fauré, Gabriel: *Nocturne No. 4 in E Major*, Op. 36

Copland, Aaron: *Lento* from Sextet

Delius, Frederick: *Lento* from Two Aquarelles

Delius, Frederick: *Intermezzo* from the opera, Fennimore and Gerda

Britten, Benjamin: *Rhapsody* from Double Concerto in B Minor

Kodaly, Zoltán: *Adagio for Viola and Piano*

Brahms, Johannes: *Symphony No. 3, 2nd movement*

Górecki, Henryk: *Three Pieces in the Old Style for String Orchestra*

SERENITY AND TRANQUILITY

Part, Arvo: *Cantus in Memory of Benjamin Britten*

Part, Arvo: *Tabula Rasa*

Part, Góreki, Tavener: any of their choral music pieces

Rautavaara, Einojuhani: *Tranquillo* from Piano Concerto No. 3

Rautavaara, Einojuhani: *Autumn Gardens*

Rautavaara, Einojuhani: *Symphony No. 7* (Angel of Light), 1st and 3rd movements

Satie, Erik: *Three Gymnopédies*

Sisask, Urmas: *Oremus from Gloria Patri*

Sibelius, Jean: *The Swan of Tuonela*

Paulus, Stephen: *Meditations of Li Po*

Shostakovich, Dmitry: *Largo* from Symphony No. 5

Satoh, Somei: *Homa*

Yoshimatsu, Takashi: *Threnody to Toki*, Op. 12

Bruckner, Anton: *Symphony No. 8*, 3rd movement

Kodaly, Zoltán: *Sonata for Solo Cello*

Khachataurian, Aram: *Adagio* from Gayane Ballet Suite

Marshall, Ingram: *Kingdom Come*

Ravel, Maurice: *Gaspard de la Nuit*

Guy, Barry: *Ceremony*

Hovhanness, Alan: *Alleluia and Fugue for String Orchestra*

Bryars, Gavin: *The Archangel Trip*

Copland, Aaron: *Four Motets*

Barber, Samuel: *Reincarnations*

Rouse, Chris: *Anhran* (Song) from Flute Concerto

VITALITY AND EXUBERANCE

Schuman, William: *New England Triptych*, 1st movement

Hindemith, Paul: *Mathis der Maler*

Diamond, David: *Allegro* and *Adagio* from Rounds for
String Orchestra

Stravinsky, Igor: The Rite of Spring

Bridge, Frank: *Sir Roger de Coverley*,(a Christmas Dance
for String Orchestra)

Danielpour, Richard: *Toward the Splendid City*

Bach, Johann Sebastian: *Toccata and Fugue in D Minor*

Adams, John: *The Chairman Dances*

Meyer, Edgar: *Violin Concerto*

Rachmaninoff, Sergei: *The Isle of the Dead*

McCauley, William: *Five Minatures for Flute and Strings*

Bartók, Béla: *Divertmento*

Bartók, Béla: *Romanian Folk Dances*

Lutoslawski, Witold: *Mala Suite (Little Suite)*

Williams, John: *The Five Sacred Trees* (Concerto for Bassoon and Orchestra), 1st and 3rd movements

Debussy, Claude: *La Mer*

Fine, Irving: *Partita for Wind Quintet*

Rodrigo, Joaquín: *Adagio* from Concierto de Aranjuez for Guitar and Orchestra

Copland, Aaron: *Symphony No. 3*

Copland, Aaron: *Billy the Kid*

Harris, Roy: *Symphony No. 3*

Williams, Ralph Vaughan: *Fantasia on a Theme by Thomas Tallis*

Williams, Ralph Vaughan: *Symphony No. 3* (Pastoral)

Williams, Ralph Vaughan: *Symphony No. 5 in D Major*

Mahler, Gustav: *Symphony No. 1*

Barber, Samuel: *Summer Music for Wind Quintet*

Barber, Samuel: *Capricorn Concerto*

Barber, Samuel: *Medea's Dance of Vengeance*

Ravel, Maurice: *La Valse*

Ravel, Maurice: *Le Tombeau de Couperin*

Tüür, Erkki-Sven: *String Quartet*

Turina, Joaquín: *Trio No. 1*, Op. 35

Alvarez, Javier: *Metro Chabacano*

Ravel, Maurice: *Une Barque Sur L'Océan*

Larson, Libby: *Missa Gaia* (Mass for the Earth)

Britten, Benjamin: *Variations on a Theme of Frank Bridge*

MYSTERY AND THE EXOTIC

Danielpour, Richard: *Celestial Night*, 2nd movement

Maw, Nicholas: Violin Concerto

Coleman, Dan: *Long Ago, This Radiant Day*

Britten, Benjamin: *String Quartet No. 2 in C Major*, Op. 36

Corigliano, John: *Elegy for Orchestra*

Carpenter, John Alden: *Sea Drift*

Kernis, Aaron Jay: *Symphony in Waves*

Silvestrov, Valentin: *Dedication*

Adams, John: *Tromba Lontana and Harmoniel*

Rautauvaara, Einojuhani: *Cantus Arcticus*

Amram, David: *Triple Concerto*

Hovhanness, Alan: *Lousadzak*

De Falla, Manuel: *Nights in the Gardens of Spain*

Koechlin, Charles: *Les Bandar-Log*

Gould, Morton: *Fall River Legend*

Holst, Gustav: *Venus* and *Saturn* from *The Planets*

Tüür, Erkki-Sven: *Insula Deserta*

Vasks, Peteris: *String Quartet No. 2* (Sommer Gesänger)

Walton, William: *Moderato* from Cello Concerto

Prokofiev, Sergei: any of his piano concertos

Piston, Walter: *The Incredible Flutist*

AND FOR THE MORE ADVENTUROUS. . .

Takemitsu, Toru: *Dream Window* and *Spirit Garden*

Adams, John: *Eros Piano*

Webern, Anton: *Passacaglia for Orchestra*

Messiaen, Olivier: *Les Offrandes Oubliées*

Ives, Charles: *The Unanswered Question*

Mcguire, Edward: *Calcagus*

Also from DeVorss Publications

Harmony Begins in the Soul,
Long Before the First Note is Played

JUST BEING AT THE PIANO merges piano theory and lessons with the spirit of Buddhism, creating a mindful experience that releases music not from the music book, but instead from the soul for the world to hear. MILDRED PORTNEY CHASE (1921–1991) studied at Julliard with famed Russian pianist and piano teacher, Josef Lhevinne. She then taught piano at the Los Angeles Conservatory and the University of Southern California Graduate School of Music.

9780875168937 Trade Paperback 120pg $14.95

" . . JUST BEING AT THE PIANO works toward developing the musician's sensory awareness of the sound, of the touch, of what the entire body is experiencing, so that each tone may sing."

~ LEE STRASBERG

DeVorss Publications
www.devorss.com